dedication

To all devoted teachers everywhere:
your dedication and hard work are
immeasurable; your influence on the
lives of children, monumental.

contents

teaching interpretation
Using Text-Based Evidence to Construct Meaning

SONJA CHERRY-PAUL

DANA JOHANSEN

Foreword by Lucy Calkins

HEINEMANN
Portsmouth, NH

Heinemann
361 Hanover Street
Portsmouth, NH 03801–3912
www.heinemann.com

Offices and agents throughout the world

The authors and publisher wish to thank those who have generously given permission to reprint borrowed material:

Excerpts from *A Nation's Hope: The Story of Boxing Legend Joe Louis* by Matt de la Peña. Copyright © 2011 by Matt de la Peña, text. Used by permission of Dial Books for Young Readers, a division of Penguin Group (USA) LLC.

Library of Congress Cataloging-in-Publication Data
Cherry-Paul, Sonja.
    Teaching interpretation : using text-based evidence to construct meaning / Sonja Cherry-Paul and Dana Johansen.
        p.   cm.
    Includes bibliographical references.
    ISBN 978-0-325-05086-7
    1. Reading comprehension.   2. Children—Books and reading.   3. Education—Standards—United States.   I. Johansen, Dana.   II. Title.
    LB1050.45.C442 2014
    372.47—dc23   2013047429

Editor: Holly Kim Price
Production: Hilary Goff
Cover and interior designs: Suzanne Heiser
Typesetter: Cape Cod Compositors, Inc.
Manufacturing: Steve Bernier

Printed in the United States of America on acid-free paper

18 17 16 15 14 VP 1 2 3 4 5

Chapter 3 Multiple Perspectives: Examining and Understanding Multiple Points of View   70

Chapter 4 Symbolism: Reading Signs and Symbols   102

foreword

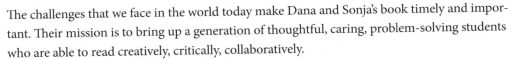

The challenges that we face in the world today make Dana and Sonja's book timely and important. Their mission is to bring up a generation of thoughtful, caring, problem-solving students who are able to read creatively, critically, collaboratively.

Let's face it. Until this book arrived on the scene, there's not been a lot of support for teachers who want to lift their students' abilities to analyze, synthesize, and interpret literature and information texts. Sure, the printing presses have been busy producing so-called Common Core curriculum, but most of that curriculum has resembled test prep more than teaching toward the ambitious new goals of the Common Core.

How glad I am that this book has arrived on the scene! It reminds us that teaching towards the Common Core can be some of the most demanding, significant, and bold work you could possibly do. This book essentially invites you to join the study group that Dana and Sonja have had with each other for years—a study group that has led them to develop methods of teaching that enable students to do breathtaking work. You'll join them in thinking deeply about the essential literary elements—about figurative language, mood, perspective, symbolism, theme, and more. With Dana and Sonja, you'll ask, "What does it *really* mean to read with this literary element in mind? How can we make this accessible and important for our kids?" You'll join these two extraordinary teachers in demythologizing the essential skills of Common Core aligned reading, and in teaching those skills in such a way that students own them.

Dana and Sonja will not only support you to teach towards the ambitious, powerful goals of the CCSS, they will also show you how to help readers bring their own experiences to texts, reading with a deep level of personal engagement. And they will help you to teach in ways that lead students to own their own learning.

Know from the start that this is a book for teachers who embrace the challenge of teaching for the 21st century. Dana and Sonja have been mentoring me in coming to understand the power of digital literacy and of tech-rich literacy instruction, and this book does out-of-the-box work on that frontier that dazzles me. But when I say the book supports 21st-century literacy I do not refer only to the fact that it's breaking new ground in digital literacy. I also refer to the fact that Dana and Sonja are crystal clear about the fact that increasingly, the role of a literacy teacher needs to be to empower students to be active agents of their own learning. There was a time when the role of a teacher was to impart knowledge—now one click takes us to the entire Library of Congress. What is important now is learning to use knowledge—to sort, question, rank, synthesize, interpret, and to apply knowledge.

In the pages of this book, you can feel, and be re-inspired by, these two brilliant young women who are still head over heels in love with teaching and with kids. At the same time that they offer us inspiration and grounding in their very best teaching ideas, they also offer the very practical details, procedures, and materials needed for day-to-day, high-caliber teaching—the support so many of us desperately need to do our jobs even more than we have before.

—Lucy Calkins

acknowledgments

On our first night of classes at Teachers College, we sat down next to each other. The rest, as they say, is history. We've been friends ever since. Writing partners, doctoral students, and now co-authors, we love learning from each other. When people ask us what it's like to write a book together, we say, "It's the best part of our week!" Why? We laugh, we vent, we agonize over how to teach certain concepts, but mostly we learn from each other, and that makes us better teachers. We feel so lucky to have found each other. This book is a product of our collaboration and our drive to continually hone our teaching practices.

Along our journey there have been many people who have inspired us. First, we would like to thank Lucy Calkins, our mentor and advisor at Teachers College. We are immeasurably blessed to have the opportunity to learn from you. From the moment we took a course with you, our lives were changed. We finally felt that there was a place where our work and interests were truly valued. Thank you for the numerous opportunities you've given us and for your encouragement. You understand the hard work of classroom teachers everywhere, and your belief in the importance of being a practitioner motivates us to continue doing the work we're doing.

Thank you to all of our students for helping us with this book! You were there with us from the beginning of this journey, and as you grew as readers and writers, we grew too. We are so proud of you, and we want this book to serve as a commemoration of your accomplishments.

Thank you to the parents, administrators, and colleagues who have supported our work. We love what we do each day and feel so fortunate to work at schools that support us wholeheartedly.

To our writing group at Teachers College, Joanne Marciano and Tara Lencl, we cannot thank you enough for your support and friendship.

Thank you to Hilary Goff, Elisia Brodeur, Suzanne Heiser, Sarah Fournier, Brett Whitmarsh, Kim Cahill, and everyone at the Heinemann family for your expertise, talents, and the significant roles you've played to bring this book to life. Finally, we would like to thank our editor, Holly Kim Price, whose encouragement and belief in our work has never wavered. Thank you for everything!

From Sonja:

I am boundlessly grateful to you, Frank, for your endless love, support, and encouragement. You are the armor that protects me and my dreams from the "too-rough fingers of the world." To Imani, my heart's melody, my greatest joy. Thank you for your brilliance, patience, and for always making me smile. To my parents, Edward and Mary, thanks for all of your love and for being proud of me. To Eddie, the best big brother a little sister could ever hope for. Thanks for always being the coolest guy in the room and for being my friend. Thank you to all of my family for your support and for being so understanding of my schedule that too often keeps me away. You are always in my thoughts and prayers.

Thank you to my advisor, Tom Hatch, for helping me navigate through my coursework at Teachers College and for your encouragement. To Michelle Knight and Lalitha Vasudevan for your brilliance, laughter, and guidance. Thank you to The Jane Addams Children's Book Award Committee members for the hard work you do to acknowledge talented authors and illustrators who create amazing books for children about social justice.

To my BIDGs: Carolyn Denton, Erica Finegan, and Jocelyn Perez, I am truly blessed to be in your company, both professionally and personally. Thank you for helping me to find balance among the chaos, for incredible conversations rich with laughter and lessons learned, and for nurturing our circle of *readerly* joy. And to Melissa Garcia, Cathy Gigantino, Abbe Hocherman, Michelle Kaczmarek, Shari Kavanagh, Jackie Marcus, Jenice Mateo-Toledo, and Suzanne Vaccaro. You are each incredible educators and women who profoundly influence, inspire, and challenge me.

To Farragut Middle School and Gail Kipper, thank you for your guidance and for supporting my growth as an educator. Thank you to all of my colleagues. It is an honor to work with you!

From Dana:

I thank my family, friends, and colleagues who have supported my teaching journey and doctoral work. Mom, thank you for encouraging me every step of the way and for always getting excited. Creative, smart, and talented, you will always be the woman I aspire to become. Dad, thank you for consistently reading aloud to me as a kid and nurturing my love for reading. *Rainbow Brite, Nancy Drew,* and *The Bobbsey Twins* continue to be my lifelong companions. Steve and Kathy, I know I don't say it enough, but I am so lucky to have you both in my life. Your guidance and support over the years has been immeasurable, and I have always felt blessed to call you my parents. Bonnie, Erin, and Nick, thank you for being my best friends, my sounding boards, and my reality checks.

To Marjorie Siegel, my advisor at Teachers College, thank you for opening the door to the world of New Literacies and supporting my work with technology. I am so grateful for your guidance and wisdom.

To Greenwich Academy, Molly King and Becky Walker, thank you for supporting my growth as an educator. Jeanette Tyndall, Melissa Wilson, Ugina Covington, and JoAnne Vicido-mini, you are four remarkable educators whose mentorship and advice has helped me to learn and grow as a teacher; I cannot thank you enough. To my Group V team, Connie Blunden, Mariana Keels, Maureen Mooney, Yumi Nakanishi, Jeff Schwartz, Leesa Singleton, and Fay Venetsanos, thank you for all our conversations about literacy, learning, and technology! And to Julie FitzPatrick, whose chocolate chip cookies are the best in the universe, thank you for always listening and supporting me.

And lastly, to my intern teachers. I am so blessed and honored to have had the opportunity to work with each of you. The years we spent teaching together remain the most formative of my career, and for that I will always be grateful. You are outstanding educators, and I feel so fortunate to call each of you a friend and colleague. Your passion for teaching, love of learning, and courage to take risks has inspired me to do the same. Thank you for learning and growing with me Meagan Jones, Nina Phillips, Susan Burns, Caitlyn Bertoncin, Sarah Bayzick, Devan FitzPatrick, and Nicole DeRosa.

Introduction:
What Is Interpretation?
Demystifying the Process
of Interpretation

One May morning, in Sonja's fifth-grade classroom, book clubs were meeting as part of a study of historical fiction. As she walked from group to group, she paused by one book club to listen to the thoughts of its members. Sonja was particularly interested in noting the group members' interpretation of the characters and events transpiring in Roll of Thunder, Hear My Cry *by Mildred Taylor.*

A folder in her arm, poised to take anecdotal notes on her students' conversation, Sonja leaned in just as Mia was sharing her thoughts from her reader's notebook. "I think the Grangers are just bullies. They don't understand what it feels like to be picked on."

"Yeah, I totally agree. They're just wrong and hateful," Evan responded.

As she was listening, Sonja noted that Mia and Evan were both paraphrasing previously shared ideas and reactions to the text. The conversation seemed to echo other discussions within the group over the past week. The students were inferring the characters' feelings and empathizing with the Logan family; however, they were not building from this to consider deeper issues embedded in the text. Then Leo took his turn, reading from his reader's notebook:

"The society in which the Logans live is dominated not by laws and their enforcement or human decency, but by people who have lots of unfairly gained power who seem to have no regard for the law or human decency and are willing to take violent action to remain in their positions of power. Papa and Hammer are courageous and willing to fight back against their oppressors. Mama, however, wishes simply to 'play it safe.' She thinks that although the Wallaces, Grangers, and many

other powerful people in their area are very unjust, the Logans don't have justice on their side because there is no real justice in their community."

As Leo finished, Sonja realized her mouth was hanging open. This was it! This was the true work of interpretation! She glanced at the rest of the group, not at all surprised to see similar expressions on the other students' faces. Everyone was impressed with Leo's response. However, instead of encouraging discussion, it silenced the group. It was almost as if Leo's thinking was so high it was unattainable for his fellow group members. The conversation quickly returned to other members paraphrasing their ideas and reactions to the text.

Later, after the students had been dismissed, Sonja realized Leo's thinking was still on her mind. She met with Dana to talk about the reader's workshop that day. Dana relayed similar experiences in her classroom. Together, they wondered how they could narrow the gap between students like Leo and the rest of their students. Or, better yet, how they could support classrooms where Leo's work with interpreting a text was the rule, not the exception? How could they make sure that this thinking was not a question of chance but was achieved by design and was accessible to all readers?

As classroom teachers, we understand that interpretation can be a murky, vague concept. Interpretation acts as a huge umbrella for different ideas and skills. And, just like other teachers, we have been unsure of how to teach our students to interpret texts, thereby leaving them to somehow learn to do it on their own. But with the Common Core calling for students to take part in the rich and rigorous work of interpretation, it is necessary for all teachers to learn how to teach this important work in ways that will reach all learners. This raises questions: What does *interpretation* really mean? What does it look like in a classroom? How can we effectively teach all of our students to be successful at constructing interpretations, no matter their age or reading level?

Interpretation is a critical-thinking process. It begins with students generating ideas, drafting theories supported by text evidence, and creating a claim or a thesis statement. Then they move through an iterative cycle of revising and testing their claims. This involves finding the strongest text support and seeing how their claims exist outside the context of a singular text, such as across texts, across artistic mediums, and in the world. This book will benefit classroom teachers as we take on the challenge of teaching our students how to construct, revise, and test their interpretations.

Interpretation Demystified

The work of interpretation can seem daunting and undefined; teachers can be unsure how to teach students to interpret what they read. Like other teachers, we've asked, "What *is* interpretation? What does it look like? If the concept of interpretation remains elusive, how can we effectively teach it?" Think about the times we've called on students, listened to their interpretations, and responded, "That's interesting" or "I've never thought about it that way." Often, what's really happening is that the student has offered an interpretation that is wild and unfounded, and as teachers, we just don't know what to do about it. So we simply accept our students' ideas. As a result, our students may come to believe that the work of interpretation is about concocting "out-of-the-box" answers in order to receive their teacher's praise and validation of original ideas. This reinforces the belief that the work of interpretation is simply about pulling ideas out of thin air.

At the same time, Lucy Calkins (2010) observes that, "In the name of teaching interpretation, too many readers have been silenced by the message that there is one right interpretation in a text" (p. 3). In short, the goal is to strike a balance between reason and imagination without dousing the flame of originality within our students. Stephanie Harvey and Anne Goudvis (2000) help us to see that the process of constructing interpretations is a creative and active process. "Like writing, reading is an act of composition. When we write, we compose thoughts on paper. When we read, we compose meaning in our minds. Thoughtful, active readers use the text to stimulate their own thinking and to engage with the mind of the writer" (p. 14). Donna Santman (2005) emphasizes the importance of viewing the work of interpretation as a continuum. This means that, as teachers, we should avoid the trap of either of two extremes: *one* singular interpretation of a text or *any* interpretation of a text. Instead, we want to acknowledge that there can be several interpretations of a text, and as teachers we must guide our students to consider which evidence best supports and justifies their ideas. Rather than asking students to come to an interpretation quickly, it helps to envision this as an iterative process that involves them grappling with ideas, rethinking, changing their minds, mulling over their ideas and those of their peers, and negotiating among the most plausible ideas before constructing an interpretation.

To further our understanding of this process, we have drawn upon the significant work of educational researchers such as Lucy Calkins, Richard Allington, Ellin Keene, Irene C. Fountas, Gay Su Pinnell, Randy and Katherine Bomer, Stephanie Harvey, Kylene Beers, Robert Probst, Chris Lehman, Kate Roberts, and others whose knowledge continues to profoundly influence our teaching practices in the area of reading instruction. Because interpretation builds off the comprehension work and strategies that our students are learning each day, looking at the work of other educational researchers is helpful to understanding the work of interpretation.

For example, we asked, "How is inference different from interpretation?" and we discovered that these terms are often used interchangeably. Keene and Zimmermann state that "Inference is part rational, part mystical, part definable, and part beyond definition" (1997, p. 148), illustrating the complexity of defining and teaching inference. Inference, as well as interpretation, involves going beyond the literal meaning of a text—noticing *how* a person or character thinks or feels and drawing conclusions about an issue or idea without the author stating it outright. "Inferences spring from the language a writer uses" (Fountas and Pinnell 2006, p. 56) and combine with the readers' ability to put the pieces together using their prior knowledge and schema to read between the lines and make the implicit explicit.

Although inference and interpretation are interconnected, we believe interpretation has characteristics that are distinct. Ellin Keene and Susan Zimmermann (1997) use the metaphor that inference is a mosaic to describe inferring as "the process of taking that which is stated in text and extrapolating it to one's life to create a wholly original interpretation that, in turn, becomes part of one's beliefs or knowledge" (p. 153). Here, we see that inference and interpretation are interlaced, potentially making the teaching of both concepts blurry and complex for both novice and seasoned teachers, and in turn, difficult for students to grasp.

The ability to infer is an integral part of reading and of constructing an interpretation. To help our students infer, we teach them to notice logical clues and draw conclusions from them. Our students are able to make inferences by looking at things in context and merging those things with their own knowledge and experiences. The process of helping our students to construct an interpretation is more subtle and complex. Randy and Katherine Bomer (2001) crystallize this process by explaining that:

> Interpretation draws on a bundle of moral, social, and emotional concepts. An interpretation is not merely a reaction to the text; it is the intersection of aspects of the text with mediating ideas, or lenses, available in the "common sense" of the culture. The interpreting habit of mind continually taps this well of abstract, reflective lessons from life and literature. (Bomer and Bomer 2001, p. 27)

While inference and interpretation overlap, we can think of inference as the foundation that allows readers to *tap into the well of the abstract* in order to do the hard work of developing an interpretation. Interpretation involves generating ideas, both big and small, and requires text-based evidence and a claim in order to grow theories about the text and then the world. Developing these theories includes looking at the theory from different angles, revising it, and adjusting it based on new, and perhaps stronger, text evidence. This development also includes the work of inference—refining ideas as new information is revealed. Therefore, interpretation is a critical-thinking process that is circuitous, rather than linear.

So can every reader do this work? Or can we only ever expect the "Leos" of our classrooms to produce this level of interpretation? There has been much debate within the field of reading instruction over whether "complex, unseen, unconscious processing," such as what occurs with readers, can be explicitly taught, since "ultimately it is the individual who must process and interpret the text" (Fountas and Pinnell 2006, p. 9). However, research shows that teachers can provide support in ways that help students comprehend texts and construct plausible interpretations, and that such support can help readers transfer this process from text to text.

Interpretation Framework

In response to the ambiguity surrounding the teaching of interpretation, we offer a conceptual framework that teachers can follow to make the process of interpretation more transparent for our students and ourselves. We believe this framework will benefit classroom teachers as we take on the challenge of teaching students how to generate, experiment with, and rethink their interpretations. As previously stated, we see this as an iterative rather than linear process, which means that students will enter and exit this process from various points. To construct powerful and plausible interpretations, we'll need to teach our students how to journey through the process.

We created this framework (see Figure Intro.1) to demystify the process of interpretation for teachers and students. The framework begins by creating an entry point for students to construct an interpretation (Generating). Then it encourages students to locate text evidence (Experimenting) or to rethink their ideas or their angle (Rethinking.) We have found this framework helpful for students as they find themselves shifting among these three processes. We have also found that some students move fluidly through the framework, from generating to experimenting to rethinking, while others move fluidly from generating to rethinking to experimenting. Furthermore, we have seen students go back to generating ideas after moving through the framework to begin the cycle again. These three processes are foundational to students' critical thinking and construction of interpretations, and the framework demystifies this work. It also illuminates the process for teachers by helping them assess where students are and where they are getting stuck.

In our classrooms, we have learners who experience the process of constructing interpretations differently. For example, one student, Mariah, was quick to generate ideas about texts. Her pencil flew across the page with ideas. When reminded to return to the text to locate evidence to support her ideas, she'd often reach for anything and come up with explanations for why her evidence validated her claim. It was clear that Mariah's difficulty was with *experimenting*—finding the strongest evidence to support her ideas. In addition, Mariah's tunnel vision on her one idea hindered her ability to *rethink* based on the viewpoints of her peers and on additional perspectives presented in the text. This myopic stance prevented Mariah from realizing when she was just plain wrong. So then the question for us teachers is, what do we do to help a student like Mariah, who has dug in her heels and just won't bend?

GENERATING

Coming up with initial ideas:
- Forming big ideas and claims
- Uncovering issues

INTERPRETATION FRAMEWORK

RETHINKING

Grappling with multiple ideas:
- Interrogating characters, authors, and issues
- Considering other times, texts, and our world
- Marinating in the opposite and varied viewpoints including those of our peers
- Realizing when we're just plain wrong

EXPERIMENTING

Testing out ideas:
- Locating text evidence
- Identifying how the evidence supports a claim
- Weighing and determining strength of evidence

Figure Intro.1 Interpretation Framework

We've also struggled with students who have difficulty generating ideas. Cameron couldn't enter the interpretation framework until we had done some pre-teaching and reteaching of concepts that helped him strengthen his inferential comprehension. Because we all have students like Cameron, we've included assessment tools and pre-teaching ideas to help inform your teaching of individual students. This book is designed to provide teachers with strategies for working with all students, including students like Mariah and Cameron.

The title of this book, *Teaching Interpretation: Using Text-Based Evidence to Construct Meaning,* stems both from the framework we've created and from the importance of students supporting their thinking and ideas. By using text-based evidence to construct meaning, we hope to instill in students not only the understanding that all ideas need basis and validation, but that there are varying levels of strength when it comes to textual support. This close reading work involves a ritual of time and practice. Not all textual support is the BEST support, and not all support carries the same weight. Chris Lehman and Kate Roberts (2013) state that reading closely for text evidence involves the use of "lenses to find patterns" and thinking about details and how they fit together (p. 19). Learning to cite text effectively is a thread throughout this entire book. We believe this framework will help teachers respond to the increasing expectations set forth by the Common Core State Standards.

The expectations of the Common Core for students in grades 3–8 is a shift from second grade, where students are not expected to reference the text directly. Beginning in third grade and continuing in fourth grade, students need to learn to identify and refer to details and examples from the text in order to support their ideas and claims (RL.3.1, 4.1, 4.3). In fifth grade, the Common Core requires that students quote accurately from the text to support their inferences and interpretations (RL.5.1, 5.3). An overarching goal for students in grades 6–8 is to cite multiple examples from texts and determine the strongest support for their interpretations (RL.6.1, 6.2, 7.1, 8.1).

While state standards and testing are important, the kind of lifelong readers we imagine our students becoming are the type of readers who do not simply let a text wash over them. We see reading as an active process in which readers question, challenge, and talk back to the text—all components of interpretation. We want the readers in our classrooms to be critical thinkers. Not only are they actively constructing meaning, but they are always on the lookout for multiple perspectives, including the author's, and then they revise their thinking.

As we continue to think deeply about the work of interpretation, we are reminded of exceptional students like Leo. Our goal is to cultivate classroom environments and deliver instruction so that all of our students are able to interpret texts with great skill and confidence. The book in your hands was written as much for us as for all of the teachers who have ever had a Leo in their classroom and who have experienced uncertainty about how to stretch him. Or for those of you who have wanted a classroom full of students like Leo but didn't know how to teach that kind of thinking. This book is intended to take the concept of interpretation and present it in manageable chunks that work well with your curriculum and your students.

Overview of This Book

We encourage you to use this book in the way that works best with your curriculum, teaching style, and students. It is not meant to replace a reading curriculum but rather can be molded to fit with the literacy work in your classroom. The mantra "Time is precious" is a reality for teachers. This book is designed for you to pull your ideas, lessons, assessments, and graphic organizers into the work you're already doing. As such, feel free to customize and adapt the ideas in this book to your teaching and time frame. In addition, we have designed the lessons, texts, and assessments to work for a wide range of student learners and grades. Each concept can be modified for novice and advanced readers. A variety of texts have been used in order to reach the many learners and readers you have in your classroom. Resources for these texts are located toward the beginning of each chapter (Text Recs). Additionally, we've created interactive charts that make the process of constructing interpretations more visible and concrete.

Each chapter represents a concept that we believe is essential in teaching interpretation: *figurative language; mood, atmosphere, and tone; multiple perspectives; symbolism;* and *theme.* Author's intent is a thread that is woven throughout each of these concepts. To further assist teachers in meeting the demands of the Common Core—across English Language Arts and Social Studies and the Humanities—a variety of texts have been used, including narrative, nonfiction, multimodal media, and digital texts.

In each chapter, we provide ways to explicitly instruct students on the importance of citing text, how to do it, and how to choose the most fitting or best example from a text. The work of citing text is essential according to the standards outlined in the Common Core, but we also see it as preparation for whole-class and small-group discussions, support for arguments, and claims for debates.

A brief synopsis of each chapter follows, as well as an explanation of each key component in the book. We encourage you to customize your reading experience of this book in order to best suit your individual needs and the needs of your students.

Chapter-by-Chapter Synopsis

Chapter 1: Figurative Language: Analyzing Word Choice and Usage

Authors are purposeful in their word usage throughout a text. Identifying, analyzing, and questioning an author's word choice can illuminate layers of meaning that leads students toward developing deepened interpretations of texts. Figurative language gives the text a heartbeat. When students learn how to comprehend abstract language and ideas, they are better able to interpret what they read.

Chapter 2: Mood, Atmosphere, and Tone: Considering Setting, Environment, and Author's Intent

Imagining the mood and tone of a text involves considering the atmosphere an author has created and the feelings an author wants to elicit and why. Complex texts require readers to slow down to better sense the mood of the text. When readers pay keen attention to details in the text and monitor their reactions and feelings evoked by their findings, they can begin to develop interpretations about the reading. Additionally, readers learn to identify details that enable them to interpret the tone—the author's feelings in a text.

Chapter 3: Multiple Perspectives: Examining and Understanding Multiple Points of View

Examining issues and the complex actions of people and characters leads readers toward the work of identifying and understanding multiple perspectives, which helps them develop a deepened interpretation of the text. Readers bring their own meanings and life experiences to a text, which in turn influences their interpretation of the text. Therefore, it is critical for readers to consider how their multiple identities, such as gender, race, family background, etc., further influence their interpretation of texts. When teachers ask students to read specifically through these lenses, new ideas are revealed and another layer of meaning is added.

Chapter 4: Symbolism: Reading Signs and Symbols

To truly interpret complex texts, students will learn to notice and pay attention to the author's use of symbols. *Why* does the author seem to constantly refer to the creek or the wilting roses or the stray cat that lurks by the back door? Active readers pay attention to these possible symbols and challenge their purpose. This is a challenge for young readers who like for everything to happen quickly. Noticing symbols takes patience. But the payoff is enormous and leads the reader to a new, big understanding of the text.

Chapter 5: Theme: Connecting to Universal Ideas Embedded in Texts

Themes are embedded throughout texts as hidden gems that reveal the author's deeper messages and empower students to think about the world around them. As students develop theories about themes in a text, they ground their understanding of the text within their own lived experiences. As students use strategies for locating themes such as equality, family, friendship, and power, they locate textual support and revise their claims. Ultimately, students will test their interpretations by drawing connections between themes in the text and their lived experiences, thus making theme a powerful tool for interpretation.

Key Components of This Book

This book is organized by key components that repeat throughout each chapter. You will also find charts and samples of students' work. Some of the charts are interactive and can be used again and again in a variety of ways. For example, the Constructing Interpretations interactive chart can be used when teaching any concept. This chart is designed for large- and small-group teaching and can be used with elementary and middle school students.

Rationale and Common Core State Standards Connection

In this section, we offer a brief analysis of the concept that each chapter focuses on in order to expose hidden assumptions, contradictions, and misconceptions that can cloud our understanding and hinder our teaching. We do not suggest any one particular definition of a concept, as this would be the antithesis of the process of interpretation. However, we've found that identifying some of the challenges around teaching these concepts moves us increasingly forward, toward designing instruction that helps students construct interpretations. Additionally, we discuss the significance of each concept and identify the Common Core State Standards that call for the teaching of these concepts.

Getting Ready

Preparing to teach a new concept or unit can be daunting if you don't know what your students already know or need to learn. This section provides you with the tools to pre-assess your students, as well as book recommendations for teaching the concepts.

Launching

We've often felt excited about teaching a new concept but uncertain about how to get started. Use this section to do exactly that: jump-start your teaching! We offer explanations of the concept, discussion ideas, lessons, and activities that can serve as initial steps toward embarking on teaching a lesson or a unit to strengthen your students' interpretation skills.

Identifying Text Evidence

The Common Core standards require students to ground their ideas in the texts they read when responding to reading. In each chapter, we discuss strategies to help students locate and select the strongest textual evidence to support their claims.

Sample Lesson

The teaching in this section demonstrates how you might approach instruction on a concept to help students read texts closely and construct interpretations. Although we've chosen specific texts, these lessons are designed to accompany any text that lends itself to teaching the concept presented in the chapter. Graphic organizers and student work not only provide a window into the type of work you might expect from your students but also demonstrate how to move them through the interpretation process.

The Interpretation Framework Process

In each chapter, you'll find a snapshot of the interpretation framework at work. This section includes examples of ways our students have journeyed along the process, specific to the topic of the chapter and the lesson included. Being able to identify where our students are and what they're grappling with during the learning process has been a crucial factor in our teaching. This knowledge makes it possible to move students further along the process of interpretation by providing them with focused instruction that addresses their needs.

Looking Across Texts

The Common Core State Standards expect students to notice commonalities and differences between and across texts, and even across different genres of texts. In each chapter, we've included ways to help students look across texts in order to deepen their interpretations about literary elements and authors' intent. The final chapter, which discusses theme, invites the use of text sets and therefore does not include this section. However, in all chapters, we've included different ways you can work with multiple texts and text sets to hone your students' interpretation skills.

If . . . Try . . . Strategies for Novice and Advanced Readers

At the end of each lesson, we've included strategies to help both novice and advanced readers. In this section, we've addressed major pitfalls students may experience and specific strategies to support a variety of learners, such as English Language Learners and special education students.

Additionally, we've included specific strategies to support learners who are ready for new challenges and more advanced work. You can also use this section as a brief synopsis of some of the major teaching points covered in the chapter, which are essential to students learning a particular concept that helps them construct strong interpretations of texts.

Planning a Year of Teaching

We end each chapter with a snapshot of teaching points that can be incorporated into instruction across the school year for each of the featured concepts. The purpose of this section is to demonstrate how instruction can build, month by month, by weaving in quick lessons that can strengthen students' interpretations of texts.

Text Recs

Access the QR codes in these sections for titles, authors, and digital bin resources that can support the teaching of each concept. We've included some of our favorite titles that can be used for the teaching that's described in each chapter. You'll notice that several titles are listed in more than one chapter; these texts lend themselves nicely to teaching a variety of concepts that help students construct interpretations. Further, digital bins provide opportunities for students to use technology strategically and capably, as stated by the Common Core. Students will access digital bins that offer a collection of primary and secondary source texts. Digital primary sources include photographs, interview transcripts, advertisements, and news broadcast clips. Students can interpret, analyze, and synthesize the information from several sources in these bins in order to identify themes and deepen their understanding. Instead of just interpreting sources provided by their teacher, students will independently demonstrate the ability to locate and answer questions raised or to solve problems efficiently. For your convenience, we have inserted QR codes for each digital bin that allow you and your students to access the resources from classroom computers or tablets. However, you may want to consider creating your own digital bins with the needs of your students in mind.

Resources

Finally, we conclude each chapter with graphic organizers that can be reproduced.

Figurative Language

Analyzing Word Choice and Usage

It was September, *and Sonja and her students were beginning to settle into daily routines. They relished opportunities during the day to engage in discussions about read-alouds, current events, and personal stories. One day, as they gathered on the rug for reading workshop, Sonja read aloud one of her favorite poems, "Where I'm From" by George Ella Lyon. After reading the first line, Sonja noticed that her students were scrunching their faces with looks of confusion and intrigue. She continued and then paused after reading the third line, and again noticed the confused looks on their faces. Sonja asked them to turn and talk to their reading partners about the title.*

"I don't get it, what does that mean?" Mariah said.

"What's a clothespin?" Jackson asked.

"Dirt! Yuck! These aren't places. How can you be from somewhere that isn't a place?" Mariah asked.

"Maybe she's trying to describe the place?" Leo said.

As Sonja listened to their conversations, she noticed that the abstract language challenged some students. They struggled to differentiate between literal and figurative language.

Before she continued reading, Sonja decided to share Leo's thinking with the class, and she asked whether or not they also thought George Ella Lyon might be describing a place. Sonja asked them to hold onto Leo's idea as she continued reading the poem.

At the end of the read-aloud, it was clear that students agreed with the idea that Ms. Lyon was describing a place, and conversations about the place she was describing ensued.

"Maybe it's like a mystery," Mariah said. "We're supposed to guess where this place is."

"Maybe it's her grandparents' house because she talks about her grandfather," Jackson added.

As Sonja listened, she realized what was missing. It was the deeper meaning of the text: the metaphors, the specific choice of words, and the author's intent. Sonja was struck by the enormity of work her students needed to do as readers this year, beginning with focused, thoughtful instruction about figurative language.

Rationale and Common Core State Standards Connection

The Common Core standards state that readers as early as third grade must "Determine the meaning of words and phrases as they are used in a text, distinguishing literal from nonliteral language" (RL.3.4). By fifth grade, students are expected to understand figurative language, including metaphors and similes (RL.5.4). In addition, beginning in sixth grade, students need to find the meaning of figurative language and also the connotation (RL.6.4, 7.4, 8.4). As students read closely, examining figurative language and word choice, they apply their inferential reading skills to uncover the abstract meaning of a text. Constructing interpretations about figurative language helps students investigate the deeper meaning of a text and the author's intent.

Figurative language gives the text a pulse. We want our students' hearts to beat slower or faster as they read different parts of a text, thus deepening their experience. These feelings allow students to immerse themselves in a text, read closely for small details, and monitor their reactions and the feelings evoked by their findings. As they do this, students begin to develop interpretations.

Figurative language is abstract and requires readers to use their inferential and interpretive reading comprehension skills. Figurative language is an important building block for interpretation because it enables readers to more deeply connect with texts. We see figurative language as an umbrella for literary tools such as similes and metaphors, idioms, hyperbole, personification, and symbolism. Clearly, this is not a complete list of the rich and various tools effective writers use when creating figurative language. However, for the purposes of this chapter, we discuss several of these tools because they most closely align with the Common Core State Standards. To do this, we can navigate the Interpretation Framework (outlined in the Introduction) in order to help readers slow down, read closely, generate ideas, experiment with evidence, and rethink their claims.

Getting Ready

Pre-Assessment

It is important to assess your students' current understanding of figurative language before launching your study. You can create this pre-assessment using a picture book, poem, or chapter book excerpt.

digitalbins.wordpress
.com/figurative-language

Step 1: Select a text that contains figurative language. We have provided a list of recommended texts in the Text Recs box (see Figure 1.1). You can also use the QR code to access digital resources.

Step 2: Decide whether you will have students read the text silently or if you will read it aloud. If you decide to have students read it silently, it's helpful to transcribe the text on a worksheet and write the questions (see below) at the end of the text. If you choose to read the text aloud, be sure to pause to ask questions, have students write their answers on sticky notes, in their reader's notebooks, or on a transcribed copy of the text.

Step 3: Locate examples of figurative language in the text, and ask students the questions below in order to determine their ability to understand abstract language. The following are some general questions that will work with most texts:

Your questions should require students to locate examples of figurative language (text evidence), analyze it for meaning, and speculate about the author's intent (purpose) in using figurative language. You can modify these questions if you would like to ask your students specific questions about literary devices such as metaphors, similes, personification, etc. For example, you might

1.   What does the author mean when he/she writes "_____?"

2.   Can you find an example of figurative language in the text?

3.   How does the author use figurative language in this scene?

Text Recs: Dana and Sonja's Book Bins

We love using the following texts in our classrooms when teaching figurative language:

Picture Books	Chapter Books	Nonfiction, Short Stories, Poetry
Owl Moon by Jane Yolen	*Esperanza Rising* by Pam Munoz Ryan	Dr. King's "I Have a Dream" speech
Stellaluna by Janell Cannon	*Bud, Not Buddy* by Christopher Paul Curtis	Barack Obama's 2009 inauguration address
More Than Anything Else by Marie Bradby	*Tuck Everlasting* by Natalie Babbit	The Gettysburg Address
Up North at the Cabin by Marsha Chall	*Because of Winn Dixie* by Kate DiCamillo	"How to Eat a Guava" by Esmeralda Santiago
Amelia Bedelia by Peggy Parish	*Grayson* by Lynne Cox	"Where I'm From" by George Ella Lyon
	In The Year of the Boar and *Jackie Robinson* by Bette Lord	"My Country, 'Tis of Thee" by Samuel F. Smith

Figure 1.1 Text Recs

want to ask your students: "Can you find an example of a metaphor in the text?" or "How does the author use personification in the text?" Assessing your students' understanding of figurative language will help guide your instruction, as well as your use of this chapter. As you begin launching your study of figurative language, you can customize your teaching by deciding if your students need an introduction to figurative language or a quick review.

Launching

"What Is Figurative Language?"

It is essential for students to comprehend figurative language. Figurative language is used routinely in our daily speech; it helps us express how we're experiencing everyday events, so it's a powerful communication tool. When a person says, "It's raining cats and dogs out there," there's an assumption that the listener will infer that in order to stay dry, he or she will need an umbrella, raincoat, or an alternative plan for getting from one place to another. The need to state those particular details is removed with the use of this idiom. Therefore, a good entry point for helping students interpret figurative language is to begin with a discussion of expressions and phrases that they are familiar with. For example, display the following sentences on your SMARTBoard, chart paper, or chalkboard and invite students to engage in small-group conversations about their meanings. This type of discussion benefits elementary students and English Language Learners who are becoming aware of abstract language and whose skills at interpreting figurative language are just emerging.

Examples of Figurative Language

Life is like a box of chocolates.

Life is like a bowl of cherries.

Time flies when you're having fun.

Time is money.

It's raining cats and dogs.

Break a leg.

I'm in a pickle.

Ask students, "Is life *literally* like a box of chocolates?" "Does time *actually* fly?" "Can a person really be *in* a pickle?" As students engage in discourse around these examples of figurative language, encourage them to notice the purpose, or intent, of this language. Also invite them to notice when there are multiple ways to interpret figurative language. You might model this process using the simile made famous by the movie *Forrest Gump*: "To help us interpret the simile *life is like a box of chocolates*, let's look at ways we can find something in common between the abstract word, *life*, and the concrete item, *a box of chocolates*." We can demonstrate this visually using a T-chart like the one in Figure 1.2.

Life	Box of Chocolates
• Many different experiences	• Many different types of chocolates
• Unexpected surprises	• Unexpected flavors
• Challenges	• Some flavors you don't like
• Sweet, enjoyable	• Sweet, enjoyable

Figure 1.2 Noting Characteristics and Commonalities

This helps students to see how life is *like* a box of chocolates, but it's not *literally* a box of chocolates. This simile illustrates how figurative language can express an idea without being literal and direct.

Have students repeat this process with other examples of figurative language that they are familiar with, or ask them to work in groups and assign each group a different example to deconstruct.

Authors use figurative language to create powerful images in the minds of readers. They accomplish this by making comparisons that are humorous, beautiful, or frightening and that explore the entire range of human emotions. Authors use figurative language to help readers imagine, visualize, and understand. Figurative language is the pulse of a text; it allows the reader to *enter* and *live* within a text. And, if done well, figurative language conveys and potentially convinces the reader of the author's point of view.

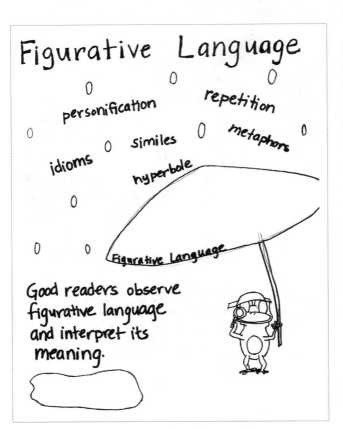

Figure 1.3 Figurative Language Chart

TEACHING TIP

Create a visual representation, like our figurative Language chart, to help students visualize the literary tools that comprise figurative language.

To help students comprehend figurative language, teach them several common literary devices that authors use. For the purposes of this chapter, we've focused on some literary devices that are mandated by the Common Core State Standards (see Figure 1.4). We provide key words that can be linked with these descriptions to help students easily remember the purpose and usage of each literary device.

Literary Device	Key Word/ Purpose	Definition and Example
Simile	Comparison	Similes use the words *like* or *as* to compare two or more seemingly unrelated things or ideas that an author has found to share a commonality, e.g., Life is *like* a box of chocolates.
Metaphor	Comparison	Metaphors can use the words *is* or *are* to compare two or more seemingly unrelated things or ideas that an author has found to share a commonality, e.g., Time *is* money.
Hyperbole	Exaggeration	Hyperbole is an overexaggeration of a thing or an event that is so dramatic it could never actually be true, e.g., It's raining cats and dogs.
Personification	Human-like Characteristics	Personification is when authors give human-like characteristics to an animal, a plant, or even something inanimate, e.g., The clipboard *snapped its angry jaws* on the paper.
Repetition	Emphasis	Repetition of words or phrases is done to draw attention to ideas an author would like readers to take note of, e.g., "I have a dream" (Dr. King's speech).
Idioms	Expression	Idioms are figures of speech whose meaning should not be taken literally and are typically representative of something completely different, e.g., Break a leg!

Figure 1.4 Literary Devices Mandated by the CCSS

Symbolism also falls under the umbrella of figurative language. However, because symbolism has broader, deeper representations that are carried throughout a text, we've designated a separate chapter to this literary device (see Chapter 4).

Teaching Interpretation: Figurative Language

One of the goals of the teaching in this chapter is to link students' thinking with evidence from the text. This will be demonstrated in the following sample lessons. After thinking about their initial claims and theories, students will discuss and write about their ideas in new ways. Essential to the process of constructing interpretations is providing a space for students to discuss their ideas. Listening to and debating multiple viewpoints will enhance their interpretations. Students will have new opportunities to generate, experiment with, and rethink their ideas about the text as they write, debate, and discuss the text with their peers and teachers. The goal of the teaching in this section is to help students develop their responses to all of the ideas they've been collecting.

Identifying Text Evidence

Use the Interpretation Framework to teach your students to identify text evidence to support their claims. If your students have little or no experience locating text evidence, begin with short excerpts from the texts you are reading, and model close reading with your entire group of students. When modeling, begin with a question, brainstorm a claim, and then demonstrate how you select evidence to support the claim. For example, take the George Ella Lyon poem, "Where I'm From," and ask the question, "How does the poem give readers an idea about the setting?" Claims such as "the South," "the backyard," or "the countryside" may emerge. Select one of these claims, such as "the countryside," and begin modeling by revisiting the text to find evidence that supports this claim. Evidence may include objects, people's names, foods, plants, weather, and dialect. Comb through the poem for all possible pieces of text evidence.

digitalbins.wordpress
.com/figurative-language

After gathering the text evidence, ask "How, or in what ways, does this evidence support the claim?"

You might consider creating a Constructing an Interpretation chart (see Figure 1.5). This is an interactive chart that allows you and your students to generate ideas, experiment with text evidence, and rethink claims. This chart not only allows you to

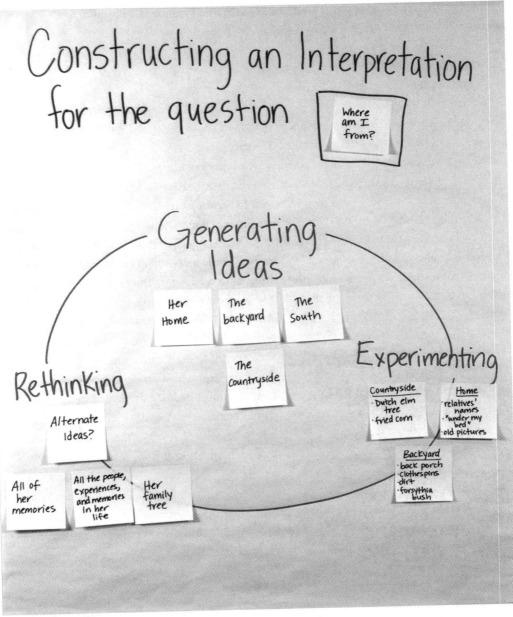

Figure 1.5 Constructing an Interpretation Chart

model your thinking, it also allows students to contribute their ideas. In the example chart, the question "Where Am I From?" enabled students to note their ideas.

- the countryside
- her home
- the backyard
- the South

Next, students brainstormed text evidence for some of these ideas. Lastly, they considered alternate ideas and pushed their thinking beyond literal places.

Using figurative language as text evidence to support a claim requires students to analyze a text. Students must pause to deconstruct the literary tools (metaphors, similes, idioms) they've selected as evidence, and they will need to demonstrate *how* this figurative language supports their claim. Central to their ability to analyze figurative langauge is students' understanding of literary tools and how they work (see the "Launching" section of this chapter.) For example, after reading the poem, "Where I'm From," ask students to identify the literary device used to structure this poem. Guide students to realize that the poem is a metaphor. Ask them to think about what the metaphor is and how it relates to George Ella Lyon. Students will come to see that the answer to the question "Where am I from?" isn't limited only to the name of a specific location, but it includes all of the many experiences, people, and memories that comprise one's identity. Therefore, students will gather evidence and analyze it by asking themselves, "In what ways does this evidence reveal the essential aspects of the poet's identity and *where she is from*?" They may make connections and links between words such as "clothespins" and "dirt under the back porch" to experiences, people, and memories that inform them about George Ella Lyon.

Analysis
This is about everything that has a meaning in the author's life. This means so many things that no one really notices, but the author sees in a new way. This means that life is different for the author.

Figure 1.6 Vincent's Interpretation of the Poem "Where I'm From"

Analysis
I think this poem is about a girl who lives on a farmland, telling us about her life there.

Figure 1.7 Cindy's Interpretation of the Poem "Where I'm From"

Whichever text you decide to use with your students, continue to have them use figurative language as evidence to support their claims, and remind them of the importance of explaining *how* and *why* the author uses figurative language. A graphic organizer (which can be found at the end of this chapter; see Figure 1.18) can be helpful for students as they return to the text to identify and interpret figurative language.

In the following student sample, you can see that Vincent is working to move beyond a concrete, literal interpretation of the poem (Figure 1.6).

In comparison, you can see that Cindy is latching on to the idea that literal words on the page are representative of something bigger (Figure 1.7).

In addition to poems, song lyrics are texts that lend themselves to discussions about figurative language, in particular with third- and fourth-grade students. We have used songs from Disney movies that are familiar to our students, such as "Circle of Life" in *The Lion King* and "Touch the Sky" in *Brave*. You can access links and further resources in the digital bins.

digitalbins.wordpress.com/figurative-language

Sample Lesson

Our goal for students is to construct interpretations about figurative language. This requires students to identify figurative language in a text and analyze it. In the previous section, we provided some first steps to take with your entire class. After your students have practiced noticing and identifying examples of figurative language in a text, they are ready to enter the Interpretation Framework and construct claims.

The following sample lesson is an example of the type of work you might do to help your students analyze figurative language used in texts in order to construct their initial interpretations. We have chosen the Gettysburg Address, the famous speech by Abraham Lincoln (1863), and excerpts are used throughout the lesson. You can decide whether you will read the text aloud or if you will ask students to read it in groups, partnerships, or independently. The following Lesson Snapshot gives a quick overview of the lesson. (Note: The Snapshot may be used with any text, not just the text selected for the sample lesson that follows.)

Reading Closely with a Lens

We find it helpful to do this lesson after initial discussions (see the "Launching" section) with your class about figurative language (similes, metaphors, hyperbole, personification, repetition, etc.) so that students have strategies for identifying figurative language. We have also found that a good strategy for students who are beginning this work is to read using one figurative language

LESSON SNAPSHOT

Analyzing Figurative Language

CCSS: RL.3.4, 4.4, 5.4, 6.4, 7.4, 8.4

Teaching Objectives:
- Students will identify and analyze figurative language.
- Students will support their claims with relevant text evidence.

Materials:
- Select a text rich with figurative language or choose from the Text Recs list.
- Select or create a graphic organizer that complements the text.

Steps:
1. Decide if students will work in small groups, pairs, or independently.
2. With the whole class, read an excerpt of the text using one lens of figurative language, such as repetition or similes.
3. Model identifying figurative language and locating the relevant text evidence.
4. Model analyzing the figurative language you have found in relation to the whole text and the author's intent (the *why* and the *how*).
5. Demonstrate locating a BIG idea using text evidence and writing an initial interpretation.

(To differentiate instruction, refer to the Novice and Advanced Readers suggestions located toward the end of this chapter.)

lens at a time. Some students may find that they can easily locate similes, but they have a greater challenge finding metaphors. Additionally, some students may notice repetition of words but may struggle to identify more nuanced figurative language in the text. Encouraging students to try one lens at a time can help them actively search for figurative language without becoming overwhelmed by the many different types of figurative language.

Examining Texts

Begin by using the Gettysburg Address by Abraham Lincoln. Invite students to read the speech and annotate it with their initial thoughts. For novice readers who are not yet ready to annotate independently, engage them in group discussions. When you revisit the text, you might say to students:

> "Today we are going to identify and analyze figurative language in this text. In order to learn how to do this, I would like you to read the text with a specific figurative language lens: repetition. Consider the length of this speech, and identify words and phrases that have been repeated. Underline or highlight these words and phrases. Keep track of the number of times these words and phrases have been repeated so that you can determine whether you believe this repetition is purposeful."

To help students locate repeated words, phrases, and images, Beers and Probst (2012) teach the strategy "again and again." This helps students to pay attention to reoccurrences within a text. Give students an opportunity to review and mark their texts. Model identifying examples of repetition in the text:

> "Class, has anyone counted the number of sentences in this speech? It's only 10 sentences long! While I was reading, I noticed some repetition of words. For example, the word *dedicated/dedicate* has been used six times in this speech. In such a short speech, why would Lincoln repeat this word so many times? I think this repetition is purposeful and therefore this word is important. I'm going to ponder over this for a bit because I'm trying to determine why. Perhaps Lincoln is questioning, or asking citizens to think

about, the commitment and purpose of the civil war? I'm not sure if this is it. In the third sentence, he explains that a part of the battlefield would be *dedicated* to '*those who here gave their lives that that nation might live.*' To me, this seems that Lincoln is reminding citizens that this war had a purpose. Later, Lincoln writes that '*It is rather for us to be here dedicated to the great task remaining before us.*' Hmm . . . *dedicated to the great task remaining.* . . . This makes me think that Lincoln means more than just the war itself. Committed to those who gave their lives for the nation, committed to

Repeated words/phrases	Frequency	Text-based Evidence	Analysis
people	3	"that we here highly resolve that these dead shall not have died in vain—that this nation under God shall have a new birth of freedom and that government of the people, by the people, for the people shall not perish from this earth"	The reason Lincoln said the word people three times in one sentence was because he wanted to make a point that the US will always be a nation for all of the citizens even after a war.
dedicate/ dedicated	6	"It is rather for us to be here dedicated to the great task remaining before us."	What Lincoln meant, was that everyone should be committed to rebuilding the nation and working on equality for all.
nation	5	"our fathers brought forth on this continent a new nation conceived in liberty, and dedicated to the proposition that all men are created equal."	Lincoln gave prominence to this word because he was trying to make a point that they are still a nation even if they're apart. In this direct quote Lincoln is talking about the promise of freedom to all.
we	10	"that we here highly resolve that these dead shall not have died in vain—that this nation, under God, shall have a new birth of freedom..."	When Lincoln said "we" he meant our nation, the South and the North will have freedom and peace.
devotion	2	"that from these honored dead we take increased devotion to that cause for which they gave the last full measure of devotion."	President Lincoln believes that to honor those who risked their lives for America the citizens should take as much commitment to America as the soldiers did.

Figure 1.8 Alyssa's Analysis of Word Choice and Repetition

the great task that remains. . . . I think Lincoln is urging citizens to be committed, on behalf of the soldiers who died, to the idea that all citizens should be treated equally and committed to the great work of repairing our divided nation—a nation divided by region, north against south, and divided by ideals—who deserves freedom and who doesn't."

We see this kind of analysis and interpretation occurring as students revisit texts to generate ideas about words used; make theories about the words' importance; examine evidence from texts that can support emerging theories; and rethink, revise, and refine their ideas based on influential discussions with their peers and teachers. Returning to the text, students can discover additional repeated words (verbs, adjectives, nouns, and even pronouns), finding significance in the use of smaller words too—not just those words that are challenging for them to define. Using a graphic organizer can help students keep track of word frequencies and begin to realize how authors use words deliberately to convey ideas (see Figure 1.8). Engaging in conversations with peers and teachers can help students to delve deeper into texts, form big ideas that frame an author's purpose, and construct interpretations of texts.

The Interpretation Framework Process

GENERATING: Some students will be working to uncover figurative language in the text. They may be combing the text meticulously, searching for similes and hyperbole, and may need reminders about jotting notes about the types of figurative language they're finding. Other students may be encountering challenges finding figurative language in the text. Remind these students to apply each figurative language lens individually and read with the purpose of noticing each form. Students may need additional support in the form of one-on-one discussions, partner work, or small-group work to practice locating different forms of figurative language. You may need to provide additional practice in order to support students' work generating ideas.

RETHINKING: As students begin to create claims and arguments surrounding the importance of figurative language, encourage them to support their ideas by returning to the text to find evidence. As they continue to discuss their ideas, remind them to consider the multiple viewpoints of their peers. Remind students to pay attention to the signals that let them know when they're wrong, such as lack of evidence in the text or lack of agreement among peers and experts.

Perhaps they're onto something, but they haven't expressed their ideas clearly or convincingly. In all cases, additional rethinking is needed.

EXPERIMENTING: When students have discovered claims about figurative language, they need to find text evidence that supports their ideas. This will require students to weigh and determine the strength of the evidence they've located. Students can use the graphic organizer located at the end of this chapter (see Figure 1.18) to record their evidence and begin creating interpretations.

Looking Across Texts

After using the Gettysburg Address, you might consider using another historical speech, such as Dr. King's famous "I Have a Dream" speech, to build upon students' learning about figurative language. While the Gettysburg Address is a good text to use to help students notice repetition and word choice, Dr. King's speech will help students learn to identify figurative language such as similes, metaphors, etc.

Before reading the speech with students, ask them to consider what they know about this speech, about the civil rights movement, and about Dr. King.

Read the speech in its entirety. You can read it with your students, or have them read it in groups or independently. You can also use the digital bin, and have students read the speech while watching Dr. King deliver it. We find it helpful to create a vocabulary box with synonyms for the challenging words students will encounter. We put this box at the top of the page for a short text or in the margins for a longer text. This allows students to quickly refer to definitions instead of pausing their reading to look up words. Remind students to make use of the vocabulary box to enhance their understanding of

Text Recs

If students have no background knowledge about Dr. King, you might want to read:

Martin's Big Words by Doreen Rappaport and Bryan Collier

My Dream of Martin Luther King by Faith Ringgold

Also see the digital bins for further resources.

digitalbins.wordpress
.com/figurative-language

challenging and unfamiliar words. Ask students to underline any other words that are difficult to understand.

After reading the speech, give students time to discuss their impressions, questions, and reactions. These responses are important to note, as they may lead to additional conversations about mood, tone, perspective, symbolism, and theme. We love using Dr. King's speech with our students as it is an example of a compelling, persuasive, exemplarily crafted text, rich with multiple teaching points.

Reading Closely with a Lens

Next, invite your students to read the first two paragraphs of Dr. King's speech with figurative language lenses. Have them look specifically for similes, metaphors, etc. Have students jot down their ideas on the text. As students begin to notice examples of figurative language, encourage them to pause and ask themselves why Dr. King used this particular figurative language. You might ask, "What type of figurative language is this?" "Why did Dr. King use this figurative language?" As students continue to read the text, looking for figurative language, you may notice that students are in different places within the Interpretation Framework.

After analyzing the figurative language in the "I Have a Dream" speech, encourage your students to read across texts by noticing how figurative language supports the author's intent in both the Gettysburg Address and Dr. King's speech (see Figure 1.9).

Once students have read, reviewed, and discussed both of these historical texts, they can refer back to President Lincoln's speech to develop further ideas about Dr. King's speech. At this point, students should have identified enough figurative language to begin constructing inter-

> Both speeches use strong figuritive language to make a point. Dr. King uses stronger metaphors and similies than Lincoln. Lincoln uses words that will unite the Union while Dr. King uses words that will open eyes about what was going on at the time. "It is rather for us to here dedicated to the great task remaining before us." This is a call to action in Lincolns speech. In the beggining of both speeches both speakers begin by talking about the past and by the end both Lincoln and Dr. King are talking about the nations future, A call to action in Dr. King's speech is for everyone to take action to get equal rights for blacks and that people can't give up.

Figure 1.9 Student Sample: Figurative Language Across Texts

pretations. Encourage students to question the decisions made by Dr. King and to think critically about the text by considering questions such as:

- Why does Dr. King begin his speech similarly to President Lincoln's?
- How is the mood and tone similar and/or different in each text? (Chapter 2: Mood, Atmosphere, and Tone)

• How is figurative language used in Dr. King's speech?

• What observations does Dr. King make about people and the world?

One way to think about these issues is to consider what figurative language in the text addresses environmental factors such as social, economic, and political conditions. Use a graphic organizer (see Figure 1.10) to help students review the text to determine what the United States looked like through the eyes of Dr. King.

Environmental Factors	Words	Text Evidence	Analysis
social conditions (how people treat each other) 			
economic conditions (having to do with money)			
political conditions (having to do with the government) 			

Figure 1.10 Social, Economic, and Political Conditions

This type of graphic organizer encourages students to comb through the text to find words, phrases, and text evidence that support their analysis. A completed graphic organizer enables students to construct analyses like the ones below.

> Dr. King observed the exclusion of black people from the opportunity of having an important role in the nation, this included the denial of getting a job.
>
> Dr. King observed that black people were being hurt and treated different by white people because of the color of their skin and racism.   ~Eva
>
> Dr. King observed the "Jim Crow laws" in place, segregated the lives of blacks and whites.

Figure 1.11 Students Analyze Dr. King's Speech

When analyzing figurative language within these contexts, students may determine that some language overlaps and can be applicable to more than one category of their graphic organizers. As students begin to notice the intersections between social, economic, and political contexts, introduce them to terms such as *socioeconomic* and *sociopolitical*. Ask them how they might define these terms.

Invite students to construct essays that discuss the historical context of the time of Dr. King's "I Have A Dream" speech. Students may decide to focus on their interpretations of the world through the eyes of Dr. King, or they may focus in on one of the words used frequently in his speech, such as *freedom*, and express newly formed ideas about its meaning, influenced by the text. Or students may take part in argument writing about whether or not Dr. King's dream has become a reality.

Dr. Martin Luther King Jr. had a dream. His dream was that one day people of all races could one day walk hand in hand, as equals. All of Dr. King's life, during segregation, he made an honest fight against segregation. In many ways Dr. King's dream has become a reality, but in many ways it has not. Now, in America blacks are equal to whites physically, but they are not thought of as equal by some. Even though blacks are equal in this country, police will stop them on the streets, saying they are "suspicious" and look them over before letting them proceed. However, in many countries other than the U.S. certain races and genders are not treated fairly physically or mentally. Dr King's dream was that everyone would be treated fairly in all manners. In this way Dr. King's dream has not come true.

Although many people may think this dream has now come true, our country, and many other countries still have work to do. For example, today in our country, and several others women are not treated equally to men. For every dollar men earn in the U.S., women with the same career and positioning will typically only get paid 80¢. In other countries women are not even considered smart enough to go to school or anywhere else outside of their homes. This is another example of how Dr. King's

(continues)

Figure 1.12 Student Essay: Has Dr. King's Dream Become a Reality?

dream has still not come true.

It was Dr. King's vision that everyone would stand hand in hand together as one. There are many simple things we can do to bring his dream closer to reality. One thing we can all do to help bring Dr. King's dream closer is simply being aware that there are some groups of people who are not "equal" to other people. Just being aware of what's happening around you may help people have hope for potential freedom. Even if you don't help physically, knowing that other people around you understand you, helps many people and races feel safe. With each year Dr. King's dream comes closer and closer to reality, but even America has a long way to go.

Figure 1.12 Student Essay: Has Dr. King's Dream Become a Reality? *(continued)*

It is important for students to understand how figurative language enhances writing and makes the writer's message powerful. Have your students articulate *why* figurative language is important in writing and why authors choose to create figurative language instead of literal language. What does it add? In the sample above, the student's writing demonstrates a close read and interpretation of the text; however, it lacks specific text evidence. This is a typical problem that teachers can anticipate, and it is important to redirect students to use text evidence to strengthen their interpretations.

Strategies for Novice Readers

You may find that your novice readers find the process of interpretation challenging, and they may require additional support. To ensure that you meet the needs of all your students, use the pre- and post-assessment tools for figurative language in order to monitor your students' progress and needs as they journey along the process of interpretation. Once you have assessed your students, you will want to identify their areas of strengths and challenges. Are they struggling to identify the figurative language in a text? Can they identify *why* an author chose a particular literary device? Or are they struggling with analyzing the figurative language? In this case, they may need to do more work using the Interpretation Framework.

Students may notice certain words that have been used multiple times within a text and think about the author's intent (see Figure 1.13). We have used www.Wordle.net, a word-cloud generating tool, that helps students see which words writers give prominence to in their work. Figure 1.13 shows examples of Wordles you might create using the historical texts in this chapter.

(continues)

Figure 1.13 The Gettysburg Address and President Obama's 2009 Inaugural Speech

Figure 1.13 The Gettysburg Address and President Obama's 2009 Inaugural Speech *(continued)*

Looking across these texts, students will find similar language and purposeful allusions to songs, metaphors, and repetition. You may also choose to create a class Wordle using a large piece of butcher paper and chalk, as shown in Figure 1.14.

Figure 1.14 Student Wordle

I think
Dr. King used freedom the most because
it was so important to him that blacks
got the same rights as the whits and
that everybody had the freedom to
talk to whoever they wanted ant to
with whoever they wanted. Dr King
used the word nation a lot because
he wanted to make a point that America
is a nation, and a nation stays
together and does not exclude anybody
and that this is the U.S and we were
supposed to act united, as a country,
and that we weren't for so many years
and he needed it to stop now.

Figure 1.15 Student Analysis of Repetition

Vocabulary plays a central role in all forms of figurative language. Ask students to identify a word or phrase that is prominent within a text and why they believe the author uses it frequently.

Once you've identified your novice readers' areas of strengths and challenges, use the If . . . Try . . . suggestions below to find strategies, refer back to the beginning of this chapter to read launching strategies, or use the QR codes to find additional resources.

If . . . Try . . .
STRATEGIES FOR HELPING NOVICE READERS

If . . .	Try . . .
Students cannot identify figurative language . . .	Encourage students to 1. Look out for vocabulary that is unfamiliar. If students are unable to note connotation and nuances of words, do some word work with them. 2. Use one figurative language lens at a time; look only for similes, repetition, metaphors, etc. 3. Have your students comb through a short text and count the number of times a word is used. If the author is repeating a word, then that word has greater prominence and possibly significance in the text. 4. Encourage students to take a small chunk of text at a time and search for examples of figurative language. A good strategy is doing close-reading work with sticky notes. Students can practice finding text evidence that they think is an example of figurative language and write this evidence on sticky notes.
Students cannot analyze figurative language . . .	1. Ask students to identify figurative language in a short text, and then have them determine why the author has chosen that literary device. Refer students back to the figurative language chart for examples and definitions. 2. You may want to create a T-chart. These are especially effective for analyzing similes and metaphors. Write the two things that are being compared—one on each side of the T-chart. List characteristics of each item. Circle the characteristics they have in common.

Figure 1.16 If . . . Try . . .

Strategies for Advanced Readers

To help students delve deeper into the author's intent, invite them to think about ways writers use figurative language as a call to action. Students can do this work with the two historical texts they've read previously, or you can introduce new speeches, such as President Barack Obama's inauguration speeches.

Students can continue to think about the social, economic, and political factors addressed in these speeches. Consider using a graphic organizer, such as the one found at the end of this chapter (see Figure 1.21), as it is geared toward helping advanced readers think through the environmental factors addressed by President Obama. Advanced readers will certainly note the intersection of these factors and can discuss this with their peers as they analyze the text.

Ask students to think about similarities and differences between the speeches they've read. Students can use the following questions to further their thinking:

As students are encouraged to return to the texts, remind them to consider multiple perspectives (see Chapter 3), along with questions that are central to the process of critical literacy. Remind students to use the Critical Lenses chart (in Chapter 3) as they consider questions such as, "Who is and isn't represented in the text?" "What kind of world is this?" "What is normalized or privileged?" "How can the ideas in this text be challenged?" and "Who has power and who doesn't?"

What is the tone of each of the speeches? (Chapter 2: Mood, Atmosphere, and Tone)

How are they similar?

How do they differ?

Are social and political factors addressed equally?

Which factors are focused on more heavily in which speech? Why?

What are your interpretations of the intent of each speech?

How does the intent differ between the speeches?

If . . . Try . . .

STRATEGIES FOR HELPING ADVANCED READERS ANALYZE FIGURATIVE LANGUAGE

If . . .	Try . . .
Students cannot identify multiple interpretations for the figurative language they have located . . .	Encourage students to 1. Return to their notes about the purpose of each form of figurative language, note which form they are analyzing, and consider the author's purpose. 2. Use the context graphic organizer to identify the historical, social, economic, and political factors discussed in the text.
Students are only analyzing figurative language within the context of one text . . .	Challenge students to look across multiple texts to determine how authors use figurative language to support their purpose.

Figure 1.17 If . . . Try . . .

Planning a Year of Teaching Figurative Language

Teaching figurative language should begin early in the school year with students in grades 3–8. Not only is it an expectation in the Common Core, it is essential to teaching other literary elements. You can weave your study of figurative language into every reading. Some teachers find that they like to teach multiple lessons (three to five lessons) about figurative language at the beginning of the school year in order to kick it off, and then incorporate one or two lessons in each subsequent reading unit. Other teachers find that what works best is to teach one to two lessons about figurative language in each reading unit, without an intensive study at the beginning of the year. You can customize your study of figurative language however it works best for you. A sample school year of learning follows.

Figurative Language Lessons Across the School Year

September: Assess your students' understanding of figurative language (similes, metaphors, personification, etc.). Introduce one or two concepts to your students. Model how to locate these forms of figurative language in a text.

October: Introduce one or two more types of figurative language in your new reading unit.

November: Encourage students to locate figurative language in their texts, and have students discuss how this language informs their interpretations of the mood, tone, theme, etc.

December: This month, focus on finding the best text evidence that supports their claims about figurative language, and have students rank order their evidence from weakest to strongest.

January: Introduce or review one or two more types of figurative language in your new reading unit. Discuss author's intent: *Why* did the author create this language?

February: Focus on annotating and close reading for figurative language. Can your students independently identify three or more forms of figurative language in texts?

March: Focus on students' ability to journey through the Interpretation Framework on their own. Can they generate ideas, experiment with evidence, and rethink their claims?

April: As your students locate figurative language in their texts, differentiate your instruction to push both your novice and advanced readers' thinking deeper using the "If . . . Try . . ." suggestions.

May: Assess your students and review the different forms of figurative language in texts.

June: End your teaching of figurative language with a review of the Interpretation Framework process.

Locating and Identifying Figurative Language		
Text Evidence	Literary Device	Analysis

Figure 1.18

Literary Devices		
Literary Device	**Key Word/ Purpose**	**Definition and Example**
Simile	Comparison	Similes use the words *like* or as to compare two or more seemingly unrelated things or ideas that an author has found to share a commonality, e.g., Life is *like* a box of chocolates.
Metaphor	Comparison	Metaphors can use the words *is* or *are* to compare two or more seemingly unrelated things or ideas that an author has found to share a commonality, e.g., Time *is* money.
Hyperbole	Exaggeration	Hyperbole is an overexaggeration of a thing or an event that is so dramatic it could never actually be true, e.g., It's raining cats and dogs.
Personification	Human-like Characteristics	Personification is when authors give human-like characteristics to an animal, a plant, or even something inanimate, e.g., The clipboard *snapped its angry jaws* on the paper.
Repetition	Emphasis	Repetition of words or phrases is done to draw attention to ideas an author would like readers to take note of, e.g., "I Have a Dream" (Dr. King's speech).
Idioms	Expression	Idioms are figures of speech whose meaning should not be taken literally and are typically representative of something completely different, e.g., Break a leg!

Figure 1.19

Repeated words/phrases	Number of times	Text-based evidence	Analysis

Figure 1.20

Social, Economic, and Political Contexts			
Environmental Factors	**Words**	**Text Evidence**	**Analysis**
social conditions (how people treat each other) 			
economic conditions (having to do with money) $			
political conditions (having to do with the government) 			

Figure 1.21

Mood, Atmosphere, and Tone

Considering Setting, Environment, and Author's Intent

It was November, *and Dana's class was sitting on the carpet in front of the comfy reading armchair near their teacher. They were eager to begin listening to a new picture book, a pre-assessment tool that would assess their prior knowledge of mood, atmosphere, and tone. Dana and Sonja had discussed their students' progress in making interpretations. They were impressed by their students' growing ability to find text evidence and rethink their claims. However, they wanted to begin strengthening their students' understanding of the literary tools authors use. They decided to launch a new study in their classrooms: a historical fiction unit that included lessons focused on interpreting mood, atmosphere, and tone. Dana and Sonja selected the book* A Nation's Hope: The Story of Boxing Legend Joe Louis *by Matt de la Peña. Dana read:*

> *Yankee Stadium, 1938*
> *Packed crowd buzzing and bets*
> *bantered back and forth*
> *The Bronx night air thick with summer*

> *The world waits for Joe Louis to take the ring,*
> *take center stage*
> *White men wait standing beside black men,*
> *but standing apart*
> *Jim Crow America*

Dana paused and asked her students to describe the mood of the text. They wrote their answers on paper. Dana scanned her students' work to see what they were writing. She saw Sarah's work:

Describe the mood of this text.

The text is gloomy.

Figure 2.1 Sarah's Pre-Assessment for Mood

Dana looked around at other students' work. She saw the same pattern—oversimplified answers about the mood, with little to no text evidence. Next, she asked her students to iden-tify the atmosphere and tone of the text. Students wrote:

Describe the atmosphere. What does the world look like in this text?

I think it's a city somewhere. Probably New York City because they mentioned Harlem.

Figure 2.2 Sarah's Pre-Assessment for Atmosphere

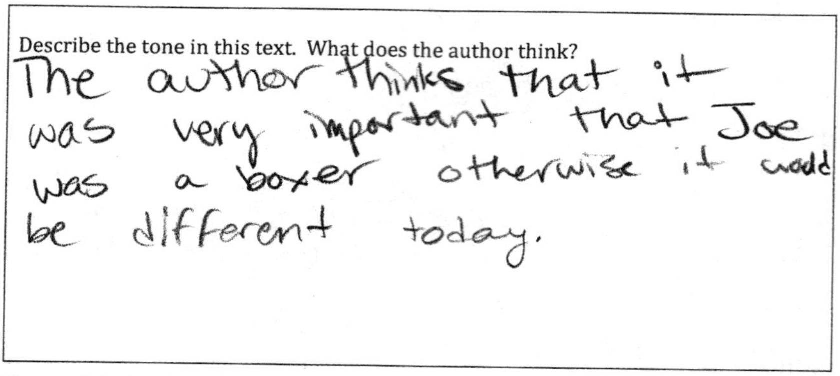

Describe the tone in this text. What does the author think?

The author thinks that it was very important that Joe was a boxer otherwise it would be different today.

Figure 2.3 Sarah's Pre-Assessment for Tone

Dana recognized quickly that her students didn't have a strong understanding of what the terms "mood," "tone," and "atmosphere" meant. While her students attempted to answer the questions, it was clear that they needed to learn how to identify and interpret these literary elements.

Dana reviewed the pre-assessments and wondered, "Which strategies can I teach to help my students identify and interpret the mood, atmosphere, and tone? How can I help them choose the best words for the mood, atmosphere, or tone? And how can I help them create strong claims with evidence from the text?"

Rationale and Common Core State Standards Connection

The Common Core standards state that readers must learn how to identify the setting of a text as early as kindergarten, and by fifth grade they must expand their understanding of the setting to include figurative language (RL.5.4). Beginning in sixth grade, students need to also be able to determine figurative and connotative meanings (RL.6.4, 7.4, 8.4). As students read closely, examining figurative language and setting, they apply their inferential reading skills to uncover the mood, atmosphere, and tone of a text. Constructing interpretations about these elements helps students investigate the deeper meaning of a text and the author's intent.

As teachers, we've heard the terms *mood, atmosphere,* and *tone* used arbitrarily and interchangeably. We recognize the commonality among these terms, as well as the nuances. Therefore, we define each of the terms in the following ways: *Mood* is the feeling the text evokes during the reading and after; it's what lingers after you've read. *Tone* is the author's attitude toward the text; it is their angled perspective. *Atmosphere* can be synonymous with mood or set apart to describe the time period (e.g., social, economic, political conditions); it's what was going on in the world of the text *and* what is going on in the world of the reader when he/she reads the text. Although these terms are interconnected, their differences add a powerful dimension to texts, one that we want our students to experience and interpret. The following lessons, strategies, and suggestions will help you use our Interpretation Framework in order to invite readers to notice the mood, atmosphere, and tone created in texts and to think about the feelings and ideas an author wants to elicit.

Getting Ready

Pre-Assessment

In preparation for teaching students to identify and analyze mood, atmosphere, and tone, you will need to assess students' current understanding of these concepts, activate their prior knowledge about setting, and help them generate a rich and varied vocabulary that will be a foundation for this unit. We can assess students' understanding of these terms by simply asking them to respond to the following questions, using a text of your choice:

For teachers who would like to use a multimodal text for the assessment, use the QR code to access the digital bin. There, you will find a selection of texts to choose from, as well as an assessment tool. After assessing your students, select a variety of texts that lend themselves to teaching mood, atmosphere, and tone. We have included a list of our favorite books that are appropriate for this work. These texts include fiction, nonfiction, advertisements, photographs, and audio clips. They may be found using the QR code shown throughout this chapter and in the "Planning a Year" section at the end of this chapter. We have used *A Nation's Hope: The Story of Boxing Legend Joe Louis* by Matt de la Peña as our featured classroom text for teaching mood, atmosphere, and tone. Additional texts are used to support the ongoing work of novice and advanced readers.

1. Describe the mood of this text. Use text evidence to support your claim.

2. Describe the atmosphere of this text. Use text evidence to support your claim.

3. What is the tone of this text? Use text evidence to support your claim.

digitalbins.wordpress
.com/mood-atmosphere
-and-tone

Text Recs: Dana and Sonja's Book Bins

We love using the following texts in our classrooms when teaching mood, atmosphere, and tone:

Picture Books	Chapter Books	Nonfiction, Short Stories, Poems
Weslandia by Paul Fleischman	*Judy Moody* by Megan McDonald	"Mother to Son" by Langston Hughes
Night Boat to Freedom by Margot Raven	*F is for Freedom* by Roni Schotter	Comic strips (e.g., *Peanuts*)
Fly Away Home and Smoky Night by Eve Bunting	*The One and Only Ivan* by Katherine Applegate	"The Tell-Tale Heart" by Edgar Allan Poe
A Nation's Hope by Matt de la Peña	*Shiloh* by Phyllis Reynolds Naylor	*Wilma Unlimited* by Kathleen Krull
Henry's Freedom Box by Ellen Levine	*Bud, Not Buddy* by Christopher Paul Curtis	*America's Champion Swimmer: Gertrude Ederle* by David Adler
Zoo by Anthony Browne	*Walk Two Moons* by Sharon Creech	Dr. King's "I Have a Dream" speech
The Widow's Broom and *The Wretched Stone* by Chris Van Allsburg	*The Giver* by Lois Lowry	Barack Obama's 2009 inaugural speech
Tight Times by Barbara Shook Hazen		

Figure 2.4 Text Recs

Launching

What Are "Mood," "Atmosphere," and "Tone"?

After you have assessed your students' understanding of mood, atmosphere, and tone, you are ready to launch your study. It can be easy to weave lessons about these concepts into any reading unit. Whether you are studying historical fiction, realistic fiction, or biography, discussions about mood, atmosphere, and tone can add a valuable layer to your students' comprehension of the text.

Before you launch your study, it may be helpful for you to review the commonalities and nuances among mood, atmosphere, and tone so that you can answer your students' questions about how they are alike and different. We confess that these terms were not always easy for us to separate, and we debated back and forth, asking questions such as: *How is mood different from tone? Are mood words different from tone words? Is atmosphere different from mood?* In order to make these concepts as explicit and clear as possible, we created a chart that explains the differences and provides examples (see Figure 2.5). We included figurative language (see Chapter 1) in the chart because it is an important mechanism for how authors convey mood, atmosphere, and tone.

What Are Figurative Language, Mood, Atmosphere, and Tone?

Figurative Language "The Pulse"	Mood "The Heart"	Atmosphere "The Eyes"	Tone "The Brain"
Figurative language is an umbrella for literary tools such as similes and metaphors, as well as mood, atmosphere, and tone.	*Mood* is the feeling the text evokes during the reading and after; it's what lingers after you've read.	*Atmosphere* can be synonymous with mood or set apart to describe the time period (e.g., social, economic, political conditions); it's what was going on in the world of the text and what is going on in the world of the reader when he/she reads the text.	*Tone* is the author's attitude toward the text; it's the angled perspective of the creator of the text.
Excerpt "The weight of history hangs on Joe's shoulders" page 5	**Excerpt** "The world waits for Joe Louis to take the ring, take center stage White men wait standing beside black men, but standing apart Jim Crow America" page 1	**Excerpt** "Black neighborhoods, Longing for a hero to call their own, found Joe." page 22	**Excerpt** "It was now more than just blacks who needed a hero, it was all of America, and color was set aside." page 25

(continues)

Figure 2.5 Differences Between Mood, Atmosphere, and Tone

Teaching Tips What literary tools are used?	**Teaching Tips** What emotions do you feel?	**Teaching Tips** What does the world look like in the text and today?	**Teaching Tips** What does the author think?
Notice: • Similes • Metaphors • Idioms • Hyperbole • Personification • Symbolism (Chapter 4)	Notice: • Setting • Time of day • Environment • Weather	Notice: • Mood • Social conditions • Economic conditions • Political conditions	Notice: • Word choice • Punctuation • Voice
Understanding figurative language means having a true understanding that *it is the way an author conveys mood, atmosphere, and tone.*	Understanding mood means having a true understanding of the *emotional setting.*	Understanding atmosphere means having a true understanding of *what was going on in the world of the text, what's going on in the world now, and how the two align or clash.*	Understanding tone means having a true understanding of the *author's perspective.*

Figure 2.5 Differences Between Mood, Atmosphere, and Tone *(continued)*

After reviewing the definitions of mood, atmosphere, and tone, you are ready to plan your lessons. First, review your pre-assessments. If you discover that your students were not able to identify mood or tone (like Dana's class), begin by creating lessons that review setting and introduce mood, atmosphere, and tone for the first time. However, if your students have prior knowledge about these concepts, review their definitions, and then go straight to the "Teaching Interpretation" section of this chapter.

Setting

If mood, atmosphere, and tone are new to your students, create a lesson about setting. In this lesson, lead your students to think about the setting as more than simply the location where a story takes place. Help students understand that setting is layered; it also includes the time period, the people involved, and the emotions surrounding the issues and conflicts. Understanding all of these aspects is necessary in order to launch into constructing interpretations about mood, atmosphere, and tone. For example, using the picture book *Weslandia*, elementary-aged students can make use of their envisioning skills to think about the main character and what he's thinking and feeling in the setting. Here's an example of the work a third grader has done in her reader's notebook (see Figure 2.6).

If your students struggle to identify the setting of a text, encourage them to ask the following questions:

If your students cannot identify the time period of the setting, encourage them to look for dates and other context clues (e.g., Jim Crow America). Additionally, you can prepare digital bins that include artifacts such as primary sources, photographs, articles, and audio

Where is the story taking place? Remind students to expand their thinking beyond identifying structures, such as homes or buildings, and instead include details about the town, city, or country.

When is the story taking place? Help students to consider not only time of day, but also the year, decade, or historical period.

Who are the people involved? Invite students to generate a list of the people in the story.

What kind of place is this? Encourage students to describe the environment or weather using sensory details and the emotions present. Also have students ask themselves: What issues and conflicts are present?

I am feeling the freedom in not having to be like anybody els other than my self, this makes me happy because its my own world and I can do whatever I want in it. It's my style of living and I dont have to wory about what other people think about me because I'm special. and It's my own way of living.

Figure 2.6 Anna's First-Person Vignette as the Main Character, Wesley

and video clips. We have used digital bins during our historical fiction units in order to enrich our students' understanding of a time period. Make sure your students are able to identify the setting as a rich and layered environment that includes not only the people and place, but also the time period and possibly multiple locations, before investigating the mood of a text. The mood is going to be based on *all* of the components of the setting, not simply on one or two of those elements in isolation.

Teaching Mood

After reviewing setting, your students are ready to identify the mood of a text. We have found that it is helpful to introduce mood, atmosphere, and tone in separate lessons. You may also choose to introduce only one of these concepts in your reading unit, and then circle back and introduce a second concept in another unit. We have found that this strategy can be effective, especially when working with novice readers. In addition, you may find that you need to teach one concept, such as mood, over the course of two or three lessons.

Visual Texts

For novice readers who have little or no experience identifying the mood of a text, it helps to begin with photographs, video clips, and music. We usually begin by using photographs of people or animals. We ask our students to look at the photographs and identify the mood of the image. You can use prompts such as, "What do you feel when you look at this photograph?" After students identify the mood of the image, it is important to have them tell you *why* they have observed that mood. What in the photograph led them to identify that particular mood? Was it the person's face? Eyes? Arm position? Posture? This helps to scaffold students' ability to find text evidence. Moving from concrete examples, such as people's expressions in photographs, to specific words and phrases in the text, helps students move from a literal to an inferential understanding.

digitalbins.wordpress
.com/mood-atmosphere
-and-tone

Audio and Digital Texts

After students have gained experience using photographs to identify mood, use video clips from movies and animated films. We have found that clips from movies such as *Finding Nemo* and *Toy Story* enhance students' understanding of mood. Again, ask students to identify specific examples of text evidence when identifying the mood. When locating text evidence, students may choose dialogue, music, and images to support their claims.

Once students have a firm foundation in identifying the mood of images and video clips, we use song lyrics and picture books to strengthen their understanding and help them gather text evidence. Students enjoy using song lyrics to identify mood, and we have found that students relish opportunities to listen to music from a variety of decades. It may be necessary to help your students locate text evidence within the song lyrics. You can scaffold their understanding by reviewing elements of figurative language such as hyperbole, simile, and repetition. After identifying these elements, students may be able to point out the writer's intent in creating a mood for the listener to experience.

Vocabulary and Word Choice

Authors choose words to convey mood. Effective word choice is specific, detailed, and clear. In order to have the language needed to talk about mood, it helps to build students' vocabulary skills. For example, it is common for students to use words such as *scary* or *happy* to describe the mood of a text. Generate lists of additional words that can be used to describe mood (for examples, see Figure 2.19). Discuss the connotation—the positive or negative association—of the word. In addition, discuss the nuances between words—the subtle difference in meaning that occurs when one word is used over another.

One way to help students build strong vocabulary related to mood is to think about connotation. Work with students to create a positive/negative gradient list. A vocabulary gradient allows students to organize and sort words based on common characteristics or magnitude. Give students a scenario, such as moving to a new school, and ask them to brainstorm words that could describe the mood in that scenario. After students brainstorm their words, have them organize their words in a Word Line that features positive mood words on the left, neutral mood words in the middle, and negative mood words on the right.

Positive	Neutral	Negative
excitement	uncertainty	anxiety
optimism	restlessness	fear
happiness	ambivalence	loneliness

These gradient lists can help students work harder to choose the best word to describe the mood of a text rather than any word that comes to mind. It's OK for students to grapple over vocabulary. In fact, encourage them to be choosy when describing mood. Word gradients can help students understand the nuances between words when describing mood. Take, for example, the words *happy, optimistic, cheerful, carefree, exuberant, joyous, lighthearted,* and *ecstatic.* Have students order these words in terms of meaning magnitude, from least to greatest. Their lists may look like: *optimistic, lighthearted, carefree, happy, cheerful, joyous, exuberant, ecstatic.* These types of word choice activities help students develop the vocabulary skills necessary to describe mood.

Teaching Tone

To begin teaching tone, make sure students have a firm understanding of figurative language as they will call upon this knowledge in order to identify text evidence related to tone. Refer to the Figurative Language chart (see Figure 1.4) in order to remind students which literary devices they should look for when examining a text. Remind students that they should highlight words or clusters of words that they believe are examples of figurative language. These may be used as text evidence to support claims related to tone. A useful way to begin teaching tone is to play Tone Charades. Distribute slips of paper that have tone words on them, such as *angry, sarcastic, snooty,* and *quarrelsome.* Ask each student to say a sentence that reveals his or her tone of voice. Have classmates guess the tone. Tell students that just like someone's tone of voice helps a listener understand how they feel, the tone of a text allows the reader to know an author's feelings and attitudes. Generate a list of tone words with your students. If they struggle to come up with words, ask them to think about tone of voice and all the emotions a person can convey through inflection and pitch. See the sample list at the end of this chapter (Figure 2.20).

Visual Texts

For our students who are able to identify the mood and tone of a text with ease, we find it helpful to extend their thinking by using photographs from different historical time periods, advertisements, commercials, and logos. Remind students that texts are angled, and that artists, writers, and photographers create images and texts that use mood and tone in purposeful ways. For example, you might select a photograph of children during the Great Depression in order to help students think about mood and tone. You can guide their thinking further by asking them to question *why* the photographer chose to capture the picture. What are the social, political, and economic viewpoints behind the photographer's work? You can also use advertisements, promotions, and logos to strengthen students' understanding of how writers, artists, and photographers create mood and tone for a specific purpose—to convince their audience to buy or sell, as a call to action, or to convey a specific point of view. Students may use the Interpretation Framework to guide their construction of claims and theories that relate mood and tone to motivation and author's intent.

A word of caution when you first introduce mood or tone: you may notice that students gravitate toward identifying the characters' feelings in the setting and label those feelings as the mood of the entire text. For example, if a student offers "brave" as a mood because they feel a specific character was brave, redirect them to consider all of the elements of the setting, not just one character's trait. Remind students that the mood is the *overall* feeling of the text.

Since it is essential for students to comprehend figurative language in order to identify the mood, atmosphere, and tone of a text, refer to Chapter 1 for additional pre-teaching strategies. From as early as third grade and then spanning across all levels through grade twelve, the Common Core standards require students to be able to determine the meaning of figurative language and analyze its effect on how texts convey tone (CCSS ELA Literacy: RL.3.4, 4.4, 5.4, 6.4, 7.4, 8.4, 9.4, 10.4, 11.4, 12.4). Once you have launched your study of mood, atmosphere, and tone by reviewing the individual concepts, you are ready to begin teaching your students how to hone their ideas and claims and to construct strong interpretations.

Teaching Interpretation: Mood, Atmosphere, and Tone

Mood, atmosphere, and tone are interconnected, therefore once students understand the nuances among them, their understanding of each individual device comes together to form interpretations that are powerful.

Identifying Text Evidence

In the prior lessons about figurative language, students learned how to organize text evidence using graphic organizers or their readers' notebooks. You may have modeled this work and had your students practice locating text evidence that they felt supported their claims. Now your students are ready to take their understanding of identifying text evidence further by weighing and debating the evidence with their peers. The following is an example of the type of work you might do with your whole class (in a lesson or in a small group) when teaching students how to find text evidence related to mood, atmosphere, and tone. Just like the lenses used for identifying figurative language, you might begin by encouraging your students to read with a lens for identifying text evidence for mood. After reading and engaging in initial discussions, students can begin to generate ideas about the mood, or the heart, of the text. You might ask students, "What are some of the emotions you felt during and after reading? Can you pinpoint specific places in the text that caused you to feel this way?"

Max used the text *A Nation's Hope*. Max's claim was that the mood is tense, and he came up with the following examples to support his thinking (see Figure 2.7). After creating each sticky

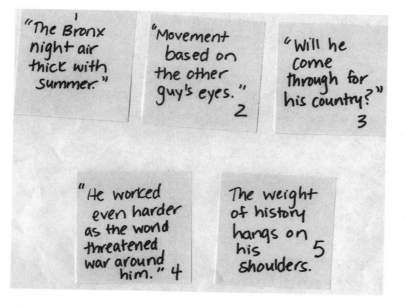

Figure 2.7 Max's Ranked Sticky Notes

note, Max weighed the text evidence by ranking it in terms of its strength. He numbered his notes from weakest evidence to strongest evidence (1–5). This same activity can be done with your class for tone and atmosphere. You might ask your students to explain *why* they've organized their evidence the way they have: "What makes the strongest evidence the strongest?" "What makes the weakest evidence the weakest?" Have students make a list of the characteristics they're using to weigh the evidence. Challenge students to think of characteristics that can be used with any text.

Be on the lookout for students who continue to struggle with literal versus abstract language. These students may choose evidence that *tells* rather than *shows*. This would be evidence that *literally* states words or synonyms representative of the mood. For example, if a student's claim is "the mood is tense," and he or she selects evidence that literally uses words such as *tense*, *tension*, or *anxious*, monitor the student's understanding of interpretation. It is not that this student is necessarily wrong, but he or she may be demonstrating an overreliance on the literal use of language rather than interpreting abstract language. The student may not understand that the most powerful—and strongest—evidence may in fact be the evidence that uses figurative language to *show* not *tell*, such as the sticky note Max ranked fifth.

Sample Lesson

Continue to help students to identify and interpret mood, atmosphere, and tone. This work can be done with any text; however, for the purposes of this lesson, we returned to using *A Nation's Hope*.

Mood

Begin by identifying and interpreting the mood of the text. Encourage students to consider their feelings throughout the entire reading: at the beginning, in the middle, at the end, and especially after they've finished reading. Model this by selecting a passage from the beginning of the text: "Class, when I read 'the world waits for Joe Louis to take the ring, take center stage' I felt anxious and wondered what was going to happen next. Why does the author say that *the world* is waiting? So, after highlighting this passage, I wrote the word *anxiety* next to it." If your students focus on only one specific part of the text, such as the beginning or end, they may benefit from using a graphic organizer to help them attend to the layers of setting, describe each aspect, and find text

LESSON SNAPSHOT

Lesson Snapshot: Mood, Atmosphere, and Tone

CCSS: RL.3.4, 4.4, 5.4, 6.4, 7.4, 8.4

Teaching Objectives:
- Students will identify and analyze mood, atmosphere, and tone.
- Students will support their claims with relevant text evidence.

Materials:
- Select a text rich with figurative language or choose from the Text Recs list.
- Select or create a graphic organizer that complements the text.

Steps:
1. Decide if students will work in small groups, pairs, or independently.
2. With the whole class, read an excerpt from the text using one lens at a time—mood, atmosphere, or tone.
3. Model identifying this literary element and then encourage your students to try it.
4. Model analyzing the mood, atmosphere, and tone you have found in relation to the whole text and the author's intent (the *why* and the *how*).
5. Demonstrate locating a BIG idea using text evidence and writing an initial interpretation.

(To differentiate instruction, refer to the Novice and Advanced Readers suggestions located toward the end of this chapter.)

evidence to support their descriptions. This scaffolding encourages students to look across a text and to consider it in its entirety, rather than making rash decisions by quickly locking onto one idea. For each aspect of setting, students can pause to consider the mood and use their previously generated word lists to select the best choices to support their thinking.

The use of a graphic organizer can help students organize and support their thinking throughout this process. Completing this type of graphic organizer (see Figure 2.11) encourages students to return to the text multiple times to mull over numerous ideas presented in the reading. Additionally, students are encouraged to see the world through the eyes of the text. This is particularly helpful when they are describing atmosphere. When describing the environment, guide students to consider not only the weather or time of day, but also the social, political, and economic atmosphere that existed during the time period of the text. A keen understanding of these factors enables readers to experience a stronger interpretation of a text. Also, students are expected to make choices about which text evidence best supports their ideas. In this way, they learn to be selective about their choices, using the strongest text evidence to back up their thinking. Remind students to cite text correctly, and hold them accountable for using quotation marks and page numbers accurately.

Atmosphere

Although atmosphere and mood can be used synonymously, it may strengthen students' ability to construct interpretations if they think about atmosphere as the social, political, and economic contexts of the time period of the text and of today. In Chapter 1, students interpreted Dr. King's "I Have a Dream" speech according to these environmental conditions. We have found that some students gravitate toward the concrete nature of these three categories and greatly enjoy locating text evidence and constructing interpretations about atmosphere. While students may approach interpreting atmosphere in the same way they interpret mood, they should identify text evidence based on the social, political, and economic factors inherent in the text. For example, when analyzing the atmosphere in *A Nation's Hope*, students might identify examples of discrimination, racial tension, and segregation in order to discuss the *tense* atmosphere of the time period. Students can use a graphic organizer to gather text evidence in order to construct interpretations related to atmosphere. In addition, you may want to use digital bin resources in order to strengthen your students' understanding of the time period.

Use Interactive Charts to Model Your Thinking

We have found it helpful to use the interactive chart Constructing an Interpretation when teaching our students to generate ideas, experiment with text evidence, and rethink their claims (see Figure 2.9).

> In the book A Nations Hope
> The Story of Boxing Legend Joe
> Luis, by Matt De La Peña, illustrated
> by Kadir Nelson there is a very
> divided atmosphere. Writers use
> atmosphere to show the reader
> what is happening in the time
> period. Throughout the book the
> author describes how Blacks and
> Whites are usually divided. The
> author says, "The world waits for
> Joe Luis to take the ring, take
> center stage. White men wait
> standing next to Black men but
> standing apart Jim Crow America."

Figure 2.8 Student Writing About Atmosphere

First, model for students how to generate multiple ideas to answer the question "What is the atmosphere?" Next, choose one of the ideas and model finding different pieces of text evidence to include in the "experimenting" part of the chart. Last, model how you might rethink the text evidence based on its strength. Do this by ranking the evidence from 1 to 3; 1 being strong, and 3 being the strongest (Calkins, 2010).

In addition, you might consider using the interactive chart Weighing Your Text Evidence to model thinking about strong versus stronger evidence (see Figure 2.10). This is a great visual for students who find weighing evidence a challenge. As you put text evidence on the scale, think aloud about why some evidence is stronger than other evidence.

Tone

After students have successfully identified the mood and atmosphere of a text, teach them how to locate places in the text that reveal the tone. Tone conveys the author's perspective and adds a new layer of meaning to a text. Just like a person's tone of voice has inflection and pitch

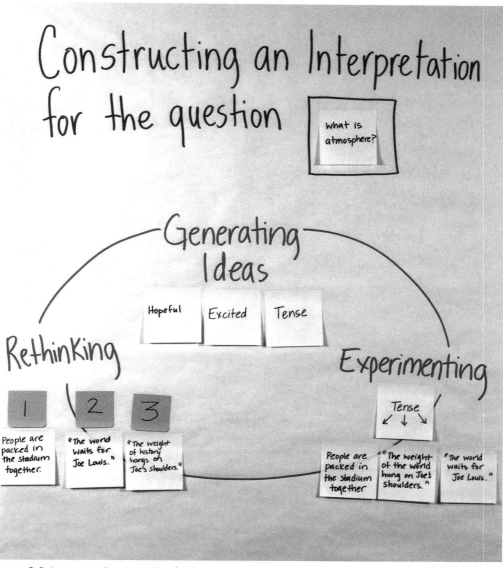

Figure 2.9 Interpretation Framework Chart

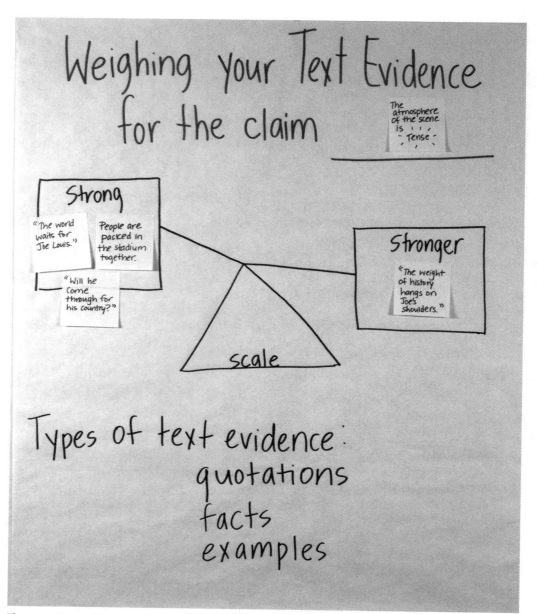

Figure 2.10 Weighing Text Evidence Chart

that reveals their feelings or intent, the tone of a text has three essential components: specific words, punctuation, and figurative language. These components allow a reader to understand the author's feelings and intent. Understandably, without hearing inflection and pitch, and relying solely on the text, identifying tone can be challenging for students. It can also be frustrating because making interpretations about word choice, punctuation, and figurative language requires students to recognize connotation and nuance, the strategic placement of punctuation, and different forms of figurative language such as metaphor, simile, hyperbole, etc. As teachers, we know how upsetting it can feel to teach a new concept to our students and not see them be successful immediately. Teachers may experience this disappointment when first teaching tone; however, it is typically due to the complexity of the concept, not our students' ability to understand it. As students practice locating places in the text that reveal tone, they will find success.

Still using the text *A Nation's Hope: The Story of Boxing Legend Joe Louis* by Matt de la Peña, tell students that they will learn how to find the tone. Say:

> "Today, we are going to be locating the tone of a text. In order to do this, you will read closely for the author's use of word choice, punctuation, and figurative language."

Model this for your students by reading the first page of the text. As you read, pause over words such as "White men wait standing beside black men, / but standing apart / Jim Crow America." Point out why you have paused over these words by saying:

> "These words stand out to me because people are standing beside each other but still standing apart. And then these words are followed by words that may be unfamiliar, 'Jim Crow.' These words seem purposefully chosen. They seem to be examples of word choice, so I think they may be important."

Pause here and highlight these words. Continue to think aloud:

> "Hmm . . . so I am going to pause here because these words are making me ask myself some important questions. I am wondering why the author is using these words. Perhaps the author is using these words purposefully to convey a message. This might be an example of a place in the text where tone is revealed!"

Encourage your students to note or highlight places in the text that they think might reveal tone. Have students try this independently or in small groups.

Once students have begun finding text evidence that might convey tone, encourage them to make an interpretation about the tone revealed in their findings. Model this process for students by having them examine the phrase "The weight of history hangs on Joe's shoulders," an example of figurative language. Have students ask themselves, "Why might the author have chosen these words? What is the author's perspective, or attitude, toward the text? What is the author's perspective on the text and the events happening in it?" Remind students that tone is not objective or neutral. Encourage students to refer to the Tone Words list (see Figure 2.20). It is important to drive students' thinking deeper if they choose tone words that are superficial or simple. Challenge students to continually rethink and question their tone words. It may also be helpful to review connotation and nuance again. When students put forward claims about tone words, make sure that they offer text evidence that supports their ideas. Remind students to consider alternate tones that might correspond with their evidence in order to make their theories stronger.

Model for your students how you might construct an interpretation by locating and identifying places in the text where tone is revealed. "When I think about *A Nation's Hope*, I think about how the people were not united. I also think about hyperbole used in the story like, 'the weight of history hangs on Joe's shoulders.' This makes me think that the tone is serious. I think the author's point of view, or tone, is that in America, race matters and is significant." The following graphic organizer is an example of the work you may want your students to do in order to support their thinking.

A completed graphic organizer (see Figure 2.11) becomes a tool for students to participate in evidence-based conversations about mood, atmosphere, and tone with their peers and teachers and engage in rigorous text analysis, as called for by the Common Core State Standards. You may want to invite students to engage in such conversations in pairs or small groups. These discussions help move students along the Interpretation Framework as they weigh and examine their ideas and those of their peers, consider varying viewpoints and possibly revise their thinking, and generate new ideas to make new theories.

TEACHING TIP

If your students struggle to locate the three components of tone, have them ask the following questions:

1. Have I located words or clusters of words that stand out as particularly important or unique?
2. Have I identified the author's use of punctuation in ways that stand out?
3. Have I uncovered figurative language?

Setting	Description	Text Evidence	Mood=	Tone=
Who, what, when, where of the text	Which words does the author use to describe the setting?	Select the strongest evidence that represents the setting.	Feeling or emotions **Atmosphere=** social, political, economic	What is the author's perspective?
Place Where is the story taking place?	USA, NY, Yankee Stadium, Bronx, Harlem	*"The world waits for Joe Louis to take the ring"* p. 1 *"Jim Crow America"* p. 1	anxious tense	reflective critical
People Who are the people involved?	Joe Louis, Blacks, Whites, The German, Max Schmeling	*"The weight of history hangs on Joe's shoulders . . ."* p. 5 *"blacks didn't win decisions Not against whites"* p. 17	uncertainty pressure hopelessness	serious angry
Environment When is the story taking place? What kind of place is this?	1938–Before WWII; Before the civil rights movement Segregation Hatred	*"Jim Crow America"* p. 1 *"Black and white Americans together against the rule of Nazi hate"* p. 4 *"It was now more than just blacks who needed a hero, it was all of America, and color was set aside"* p. 25	fear optimism hopeful	judgmental optimistic hopeful

Figure 2.11 Completed Graphic Organizer

Writing About Mood

Once your students have journeyed through the Interpretation Framework, they can write analytical paragraphs, essays, or other forms of response. In order to help your students convey their ideas clearly in a paragraph or short response, we recommend teaching a few simple writing strategies. We encourage our students to start by using "BAM!" to formulate their topic sentences or claims. "BAM!" is a mnemonic that stands for **B**ook title, **A**uthor's Name, and **M**ain idea of the paragraph. This is a simple way for students to remember what to include in their topic sentence. We tell our students, "You want readers to know your claim immediately—BAM!"

In addition, it is important for students to define the literary element they are discussing and articulate why authors use it. In Figure 2.12, for example, the student writes, "Writers create a mood in their text to help the reader 'feel' and imagine their (the author's) work better." This is important because it gives students the opportunity to verbalize why the literary device is important for readers.

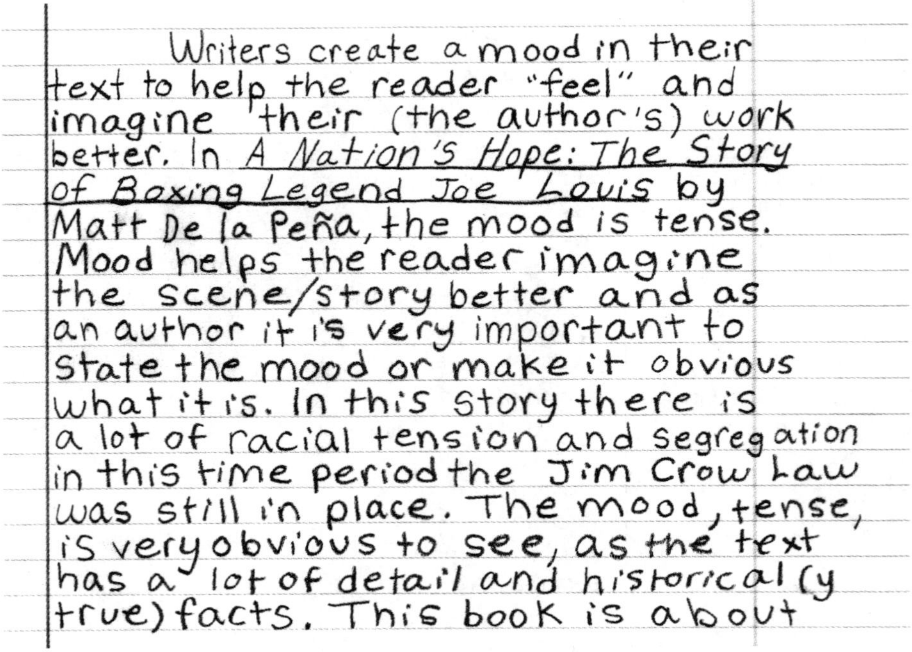

> Writers create a mood in their text to help the reader "feel" and imagine their (the author's) work better. In *A Nation's Hope: The Story of Boxing Legend Joe Louis* by Matt De la Peña, the mood is tense. Mood helps the reader imagine the scene/story better and as an author it is very important to state the mood or make it obvious what it is. In this story there is a lot of racial tension and segregation in this time period the Jim Crow Law was still in place. The mood, tense, is very obvious to see, as the text has a lot of detail and historical (y true) facts. This book is about

Figure 2.12 Student's Analytical Paragraph About Mood

The Interpretation Framework Process

GENERATING IDEAS: The process of generating ideas is synonymous with brainstorming. You may teach different strategies for this process when students are learning how to interpret mood, atmosphere, and tone. For example, you might begin by having students notice their own emotional responses to the text, jotting them down, and then annotating the text or flagging text evidence with a sticky note. In the generating stage, it is important that students circle or underline text evidence that sparks the idea for their claim.

RETHINKING: Students often need encouragement to rethink their initial claims. We have taught students who are reluctant to reconsider their first idea. It is important for students to practice rethinking and exploring their ideas more deeply. Students can benefit from small-group discussions about the mood and tone of texts. These discussions provide students with opportunities to rethink their claims as they are exposed to alternative theories and can consider the ideas of their peers, who may have a different point of view.

EXPERIMENTING: As students cite text evidence, they may benefit from using a graphic organizer. Remind students to organize and label their work by including the page number and jotting down a few ideas about how the text evidence supports their claims. If students feel limited with words they can use to describe mood and tone, create a class chart and/or handout with mood and tone vocabulary that students can apply to the various texts they read.

Looking Across Texts

In addition, it is a great idea to bring in your students' prior knowledge and experiences with other texts. This will layer their understanding of concepts such as segregation, civil rights, and racism. For example, students may bring in their knowledge about segregation learned by reading texts such as *Bud, Not Buddy* by Christopher Paul Curtis, *Freedom Summer* by Deborah Wiles, or Dr. King's "I Have a Dream" speech even though these three texts take place in different settings.

In the book Bud not Buddy by Christopher
Paul Curtis there is a very scary mood. The scary
mood is created when he is locked in a dark
and eerie shed because his new "foster" brother"
set him up so he would get Bud in trouble and be
punished. Authors create mood by using descriptive
words and repetition in their writing, that makes the
reader feel a certain mood. An example of how the
author creates a scary mood is when he writes "Each
head had a wide open mouth with a sharp set of teeth
and lips smiling back at you ready to bite." (pg.22)
That conveys a scary feeling to the reader. Also, the
author creates repetition in his writing to emphasize
his theme. In this case he wants to make a point
when he repeatedly says "He could kiss my wrist if
he thought that as good to happen." (pg. 26) Throughout
the book Bud says this three times. Many times through
the book the author generates a scary mood using
repetition and expressive words.

Figure 2.13 Student Analysis of Mood

(continues)

Authors use mood to create a story that gives readers plenty to think about. In the shed scene of the book <u>Buddy Not Buddy</u> by Christopher Paul Curtis, the mood is frightening. Bud is scared silly, though he pretends not to be, not wanting the Amoses to think they had "won". Bud is scared of the fish heads on the door, the "vampire" on the cieling, and the bugs and vermin all over the floor. In this scene, Bud is locked in the shed, trying to calm his fear. "The only thing I could hear was my own breath. It sounded like there were six scared people locked in the shed. I closed my eyes and thought real hard about making my breathing slow down. Pretty soon it sounded like the five other breathers in the shed had left. I was still scared but now it was that get-real-excited-and-want-to-move-around kind of scared..." This is important because the author uses fear, which shows a different side to the character. Curtis is no longer showing how Bud acts in normal circumstances, he is showing what fear can do to change someone. Curtis used mood to create this scene, that helps the reader relate to the character.

Figure 2.13 Student Analysis of Mood *(continued)*

Strategies for Novice Readers

When teaching mood, atmosphere, and tone to novice readers, an important strategy for locating text evidence is learning how to annotate the text while they read. One way to teach annotating is to have students use one lens at a time (take mood, for example) and practice doing a close reading of one or two pages. While reading closely, ask students to underline, highlight, or jot down notes right on the text. We find that it is good to introduce one or two lenses at a time for novice readers to try. Giving students a list of three or more lenses can be overwhelming and defeats the purpose of having them practice reading closely. Instead, it is a good idea to build a list of lenses over time. You may have students record this list on a sticky note that they carry with them from book to book, or you may want them to write the list in their reader's notebook.

Annotating Text

If students do not have their own personal copies of the text to write on, photocopy pages of the text so they can practice annotating directly on the page. This is an important strategy, not just for analyzing texts in class, but also for test preparation. Students need to be familiar with how to identify and note their ideas on the text. If your students use sticky notes to mark their ideas, encourage them to write two to three sticky notes per page as they read closely. Again, it is important for students to use only one or two lenses at a time while reading. As they build their annotating skills, they will be able to read with more lenses at a time.

What are students writing in the margins or on their sticky notes? Students are underlining text or quoting it (on sticky notes) and jotting down which literary element they have found. It will be important for you to model how to do this work with your students. These annotations are jumping off points for your students' interpretations. It is an important first step on the Interpretation Framework for your students to be able to locate text evidence that connects to a variety of literary elements. Once they have found text evidence, they can begin jotting down their initial claims.

Assessing Students

After working with your students to identify and interpret mood, atmosphere, and tone, give your students a post-assessment. This assessment can be the same as your pre-assessment, which is useful because you can compare your students' responses before and after your teaching.

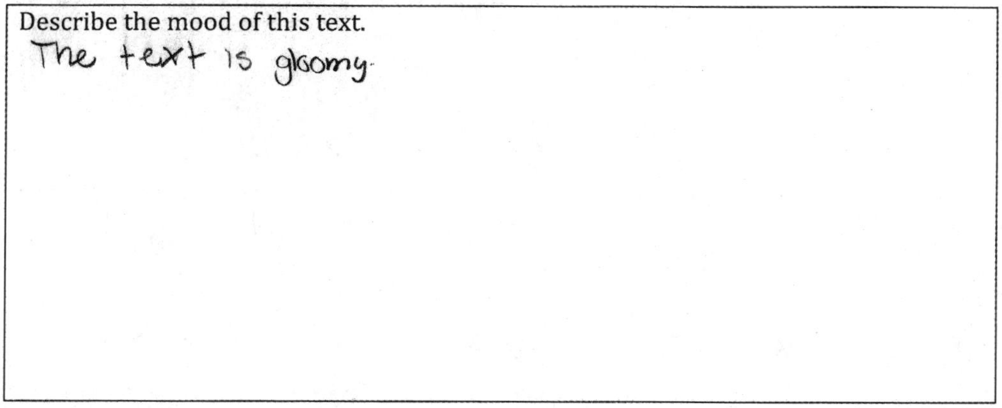

> Describe the mood of this text.
>
> The text is gloomy.

Figure 2.14 Pre-Assessment

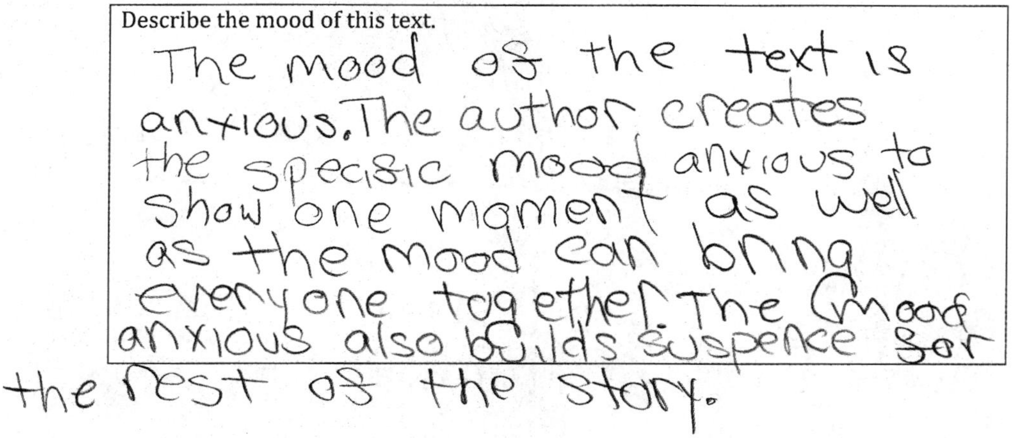

> Describe the mood of this text.
>
> The mood of the text is anxious. The author creates the speasic mood anxious to show one mament as well as the mood can bring everyone together. The (mood anxious also build's suspence for the rest of the story.

Figure 2.15 Post-Assessment

If . . . Try . . .

You may consider using the If . . . Try . . . suggestions to create charts that your students can use in the classroom in order to become more independent when constructing interpretations. Here we have used some of the If . . . Try . . . tips to create a chart that students can refer to (see Figure 2.16).

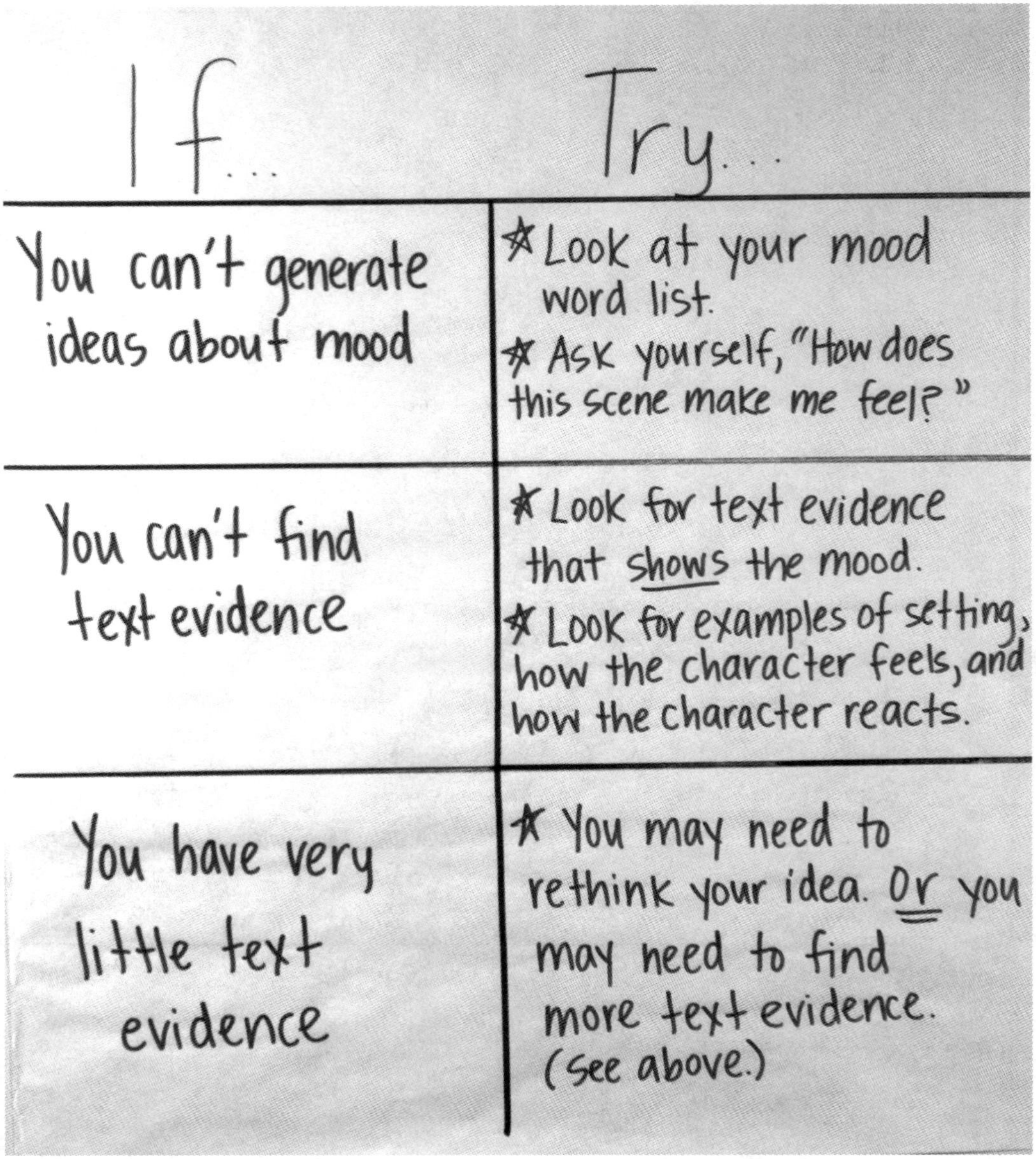

If...	Try...
You can't generate ideas about mood	✶ Look at your mood word list. ✶ Ask yourself, "How does this scene make me feel?"
You can't find text evidence	✶ Look for text evidence that <u>shows</u> the mood. ✶ Look for examples of setting, how the character feels, and how the character reacts.
You have very little text evidence	✶ You may need to rethink your idea. <u>Or</u> you may need to find more text evidence. (See above.)

Figure 2.16 If . . . Try . . . Chart

If . . . Try . . .

HELPING NOVICE READERS CREATE INTERPRETATIONS ABOUT MOOD, ATMOSPHERE, AND TONE

If . . .	Try . . .
Students are not choosing the most specific words for mood and tone . . . (You can tell because they are choosing simplistic, superficial words.)	Direct students to the charts or handouts that list mood and tone words. Discuss connotation by having students sort the words into positive, negative, and neutral categories. You many also want to create word gradients in order to brainstorm the small but important differences between words.
Students are struggling to form a claim . . . (You can tell because they may be summarizing the text, gathering evidence that is unconnected, or they are stuck in the gray.)	You might begin by talking to students about what a claim is. Prompt them with questions such as "What emotions do you feel when reading the text?" "Why might the author be creating these feelings?" or "What does the author want us to learn?" Encourage students to "try on" different lenses. See Chapter 3 for the Critical Lenses chart.
Students are struggling to rethink their interpretation . . .	Help your students understand that rethinking their theories is part of making a strong interpretation. Show students an example of an interpretation that was made stronger because the evidence was reconsidered or the claim was changed. Encourage your students to first look for more evidence to support their claim. If they can find more evidence, guide them to choose the strongest evidence. If they cannot find additional examples, encourage them to reconsider their claim.
Students are having difficulty identifying the author's point of view and connection to the world . . .	Prompt students with questions such as, "What is the author trying to teach you?" "Why did the author make this choice?" "What ideas about life does this text help us to think about?"

Figure 2.17 If . . . Try . . .

Strategies for Advanced Readers

For students who are proficient at identifying and interpreting the mood, atmosphere, and tone of a text, invite them to write a literary analysis. Encourage students to notice that mood and tone may shift throughout a text, therefore they should carefully note where these shifts occur by locating transition words, such as *yet*, *however*, and *but*. In their essays, students should discuss where these shifts occur and analyze the changes.

If . . . Try . . .
HELPING ADVANCED READERS CREATE INTERPRETATIONS ABOUT MOOD, ATMOSPHERE, AND TONE

If . . .	Try . . .
Students are finding lots of good evidence but not weighing it . . .	Discuss the purpose of finding strong evidence. "What does the evidence do?" You might want to do some inquiry work with sample evidence from your work with a previous text in order to review how the strongest evidence proved the claim. Encourage students to rank order their text evidence and debate each piece. What are the pros and cons for using this piece of evidence when trying to prove their claim?
Students are making claims that are strong but could be even stronger . . .	Guide students to make connections between mood, atmosphere, and tone. How does the author use all three elements to create meaning?
Students are forming a strong claim, finding strong evidence, but not rethinking . . .	You might begin by modeling the process of rethinking. You could say, "Even though you have a strong claim and strong evidence, it is important to always look for different angles. Try a different viewpoint and see how that affects your claim."
Students are critical readers but continue to examine the text through one lens . . .	Using the Critical Lenses chart (see Figure 3.2), encourage students to try on different lenses. How do they view the mood, atmosphere, and tone through the different lenses?

Figure 2.18 If . . . Try . . .

As students revisit the text and any graphic organizers they've completed, they should locate key words and phrases that most powerfully demonstrate mood, atmosphere, and tone. They will use this evidence to support their analysis. Remind students to consider the following questions as they write their essays:

What is the purpose of this writing and topic?

How does the author feel about this topic?

Which specific words or phrases capture the mood, atmosphere, and tone of the text?

Why has the author used these specific words or phrases?

What does the author want readers to feel, think, or believe?

What questions/concerns are raised for you as a result of this text?

Planning a Year of Teaching Mood, Atmosphere, and Tone

As you plan your reading units for the school year and select your core texts and read-alouds, it will be important for you to think about how you will integrate mood, atmosphere, and tone lessons into your teaching. We have found that it is beneficial to introduce mood, atmosphere, and tone separately, as they can be confusing to students because of their similarities. Following is a sample plan for teaching mood, atmosphere, and tone to your students over the course of a school year.

digitalbins.wordpress
.com/mood-atmosphere
-and-tone

Mood, Atmosphere, and Tone Lessons Across the School Year

September: Assess your students' understanding of mood, atmosphere, and tone. Introduce mood, and have students use the Interpretation Framework to create claims.

October: Build on your students' understanding of mood by stressing the importance of word choice and finding relevant text evidence to support their claims.

November: This month, introduce atmosphere and compare and contrast with mood.

December: Have students identify text evidence for mood and atmosphere and write thesis statements.

January: Introduce tone to your students. Model identifying evidence to support claims about the tone of a text. Discuss why the author created the tone. What is the purpose? The message?

February: Lead your students' thinking deeper by having them find evidence of mood, atmosphere, and tone in a text. Discuss how all three elements work together.

March: Have students practice identifying and interpreting mood, atmosphere, and tone in their book clubs and independent reading. Hone and deepen students' understanding of citing text evidence and finding the strongest evidence to support their claims about mood, atmosphere, and tone.

April: Compare and contrast mood, atmosphere, and tone across texts or in text sets.

May: Assess your students' understanding of the Interpretation Framework and use the If . . . Try . . . tips to develop your students' understanding of these elements.

June: End your year of teaching mood, atmosphere, and tone with a review of the Interpretation Framework process.

Sample Mood Word List	
POSITIVE	**NEGATIVE**
amused	aggravated
awed	annoyed
calm	anxious
cheerful	apathetic
confident	apprehensive
contemplative	brooding
content	confused
determined	cranky
dignified	crushed
empowered	cynical
energetic	depressed
enthralled	disappointed
excited	distressed
exhilarated	drained
grateful	dreary
harmonious	embarrassed
hopeful	enraged
idyllic	envious
joyous	exhausted
jubilant	frustrated
liberating	gloomy
lighthearted	grumpy
loving	hopeless
mellow	hostile
nostalgic	indifferent
optimistic	infuriated
passionate	jealous
peaceful	lonely
playful	merciless
pleased	moody
rejuvenated	nervous
relaxed	numb
relieved	pessimistic
satisfied	restless
sentimental	scared
silly	serious
surprised	somber
sympathetic	stressed
thankful	tense
thoughtful	uncomfortable
	worried

Figure 2.19

Sample Tone Word List		
angry	livid	seductive
annoyed	sarcastic	jovial
disappointed	artificial	breezy
dejected	paranoid	appreciative
afraid	cynical	joyous
jeering	superficial	pleasant
depressed	condescending	soothing
desperate	snide	ecstatic
sad	scornful	hopeful
hateful	mocking	optimistic
scornful	shrill	humorous
nervous	hurt	passive
haughty	confused	persuasive
scathing	sharp	merry
sharp	disgusted	authoritative
bitter	haughty	knowledgeable
harsh	arrogant	surprised
agitated	happy	content
pessimistic	excited	questioning
irritated	sweet	curious
outraged	sympathetic	admiring
sympathetic	reflective	proud
gracious	dreamy	encouraging
courteous	lighthearted	vibrant
respectful	humble	whimsical
romantic	instructive	wistful
loving	serious	
enthusiastic		

Figure 2.20

Setting	Description	Text Evidence	Mood=	Tone=
Who, what, when, where of the text	Which words does the author use to describe the setting?	Select the strongest evidence that represents the setting.	Feeling or emotions **Atmosphere=** social, political, economic	What is the author's perspective?
Place Where is the story taking place?				
People Who are the people involved?				
Environment When is the story taking place? What kind of place is this?				

Figure 2.21

3

Multiple Perspectives

Examining and Understanding Multiple Points of View

Before every reading unit, *Sonja conducts a pre-assessment with her class to assess overall the students' comprehension skills. She crafts questions around skills such as inferring, synthesizing, and interpreting. After administering this informal assessment, she sorts through her students' responses, which then guides her instruction. An assessment in January included the text* Freedom Summer *by Deborah Wiles. It is the story of a friendship between John Henry, who is black, and Joe, who is white, and takes place during the civil rights movement.*

After giving the assessment, Sonja sat down to read her students' responses. In general, she was not surprised by what she read. That was until she got to the prompt: "What is John Henry's perspective about the town's decision?" The first response read, "I think John Henry is sad because he can't swim in the pool."

She turned to the next response, and the next, only to find that the majority had answered in a similar fashion. Well, she thought, he IS sad, but what else? It was clear that Sonja's students were inferring the character's feelings and thoughts. Naturally, they could relate to John Henry's feelings of sadness because they too have experienced feelings of sadness when being left out or excluded. What this showed

Sonja was that her students were continuing to infer, but they were not yet able to interpret a character's perspective. What does John Henry's sadness mean? Is his sadness due to just one instance, or is it representative of something bigger—bigger than this book, bigger than this one reading unit? Sonja realized that she needed to direct her students to consider questions that would get them to think outside of themselves or outside of single pages of text. How was she going to teach them to steer beyond identifying the character's feelings in any single situation?

As teachers, we know that many of our students have a tendency to think of characters in one-dimensional ways, rather than as complex personalities dealing with intricate issues. Instead of students simply focusing in on the basic description of characters and their feelings, how can we unlock the door to an awareness of the multiple perspectives of characters who are influenced by the world in which they live?

Rationale and Common Core State Standards Connection

An expectation set by the Common Core standards is that readers must be able to compare and contrast two or more settings, characters, and events in a story, drawing on specific details in the text (RL.5.1, 5.6, 6.1, 6.6, 7.1, 7.6, 8.1). This means students must read closely to study and examine multiple perspectives, not to simply see the story from the point of view of a single character, but rather from the viewpoint of different characters and the author.

By examining multiple perspectives embedded within a text, including the author's perspective, readers can begin to think about how people deal with problems differently and how authors deal with issues differently. Such examination lays the foundation for students to engage in social critique. Teachers and schools play a vital role in exposing students to points of view that may be unfamiliar. This political and moral responsibility calls for school pedagogy in which social justice is central.

Examining issues and the complex actions of people and characters lead readers toward the work of identifying and understanding multiple perspectives to develop a deeper interpretation of texts. Readers bring their own meaning and life experiences to a text, which, in turn, influence their interpretation of these texts. Therefore, it is critical for readers to consider how the multiple identities of characters and people—such as gender, race, religion, family background, etc.—influence their points of view and also how these multiple aspects influence a readers' interpretation of texts. Furthermore, readers can consider how and what characters' identities may help to clarify and what may be obscured because of them. When teachers ask students to read closely through different lenses, new ideas are revealed and another layer of meaning is added to students' interpretation of a text.

The following lessons, strategies, and suggestions invite readers to think deeply about texts by viewing the world from the eyes of characters and people that may have been marginalized or silenced. Taking on their point of view and understanding their role in a story or their stance on an issue gives readers a stronger understanding of what the author may be trying to convey, and subsequently, enables readers to make a stronger interpretation of the text. When readers better understand multiple perspectives within a text, they can acquire the knowledge to support and defend their own points of view with sound arguments and theories about characters, people, and issues. That being said, this work also leads readers to discover that the world is complex. They will learn to grapple with ambiguity and questions that can be interpreted in many ways. Therefore, it's vital that teachers create spaces in which the purpose of reading is not limited to the acquisition of technical skills but shifts beyond such boundaries and underscores the importance of raising questions, interrogating singular and commonly accepted worldviews, and celebrating unique interpretations.

Getting Ready

Pre-Assessment

In preparation for teaching students to identify and analyze multiple points of view, it is important to plan how we will scaffold students' understanding of how to interpret multiple perspectives, and we need to anticipate the potential pitfalls. Begin by assessing your students' understanding of generating interpretations about multiple perspectives. You can create this assessment using general questions that will work with a variety of texts.

1. What is perspective?

2. What is the difference between perspective and opinion?

3. What is _____'s perspective in the text?

4. What is the author's perspective?

For teachers who would like to use a multimodal text for an assessment, use the QR code to access the digital bin. After assessing your students, collect a variety of texts that contain multiple perspectives. We have included a list of our favorite texts that lend themselves nicely to the work of teaching multiple perspectives. These texts include fiction, nonfiction, advertisements, photographs, and audio clips. They may be found using the QR code noted throughout

digitalbins.wordpress
.com/multiple
-perspectives

this chapter and in the "Planning a Year" section at the end of this chapter. We used the short story "The Wrong Lunch Line" by Nicholasa Mohr as our featured classroom text for teaching multiple perspectives. Additional texts are used to support the ongoing work of novice and advanced readers.

Text Recs: Dana and Sonja's Book Bins

We love using the following texts in our classrooms when teaching multiple perspectives:

Picture Books	Chapter Books	Nonfiction, Short Stories, Poetry
The True Story of the Three Little Pigs by Jon Scieszka	*Wonder* by R. J. Palacio	"The Wrong Lunch Line" by Nicholasa Mohr
Zoo by Anthony Browne	*Sylvia & Aki* by Winifred Conkling	"Joyful Noise: Poems for Two Voices" by Paul Fleischman
The Jolly Postman by Janet and Allan Ahlberg	*Granny Torrelli Makes Soup* by Sharon Creech	*Time for Kids* magazines
The Lorax by Dr. Seuss	*Seedfolks* by Paul Fleischman	*The Aztec News* and *The Egyptian News* by Philip Steele
Dear Mrs. LaRue by Mark Teague	*Rules* by Cynthia Lord	You Wouldn't Want to Be series, published by Franklin Watts
Encounter by Jane Yolen	*Roll of Thunder, Hear My Cry* by Mildred Taylor	If You Lived at the Time of series, published by Scholastic
	Because of Mr. Terupt by Rob Buyea	*To the Mountaintop* by Charlayne Hunter-Gault
	The One and Only Ivan by Katherine Applegate	*Almost Astronauts* by Tanya Lee Stone
	Bull Run by Paul Fleischman	

Figure 3.1 Text Recs

Launching

"What Is Perspective?"

Prior to teaching multiple perspectives, we need to think about how we will present the term *multiple perspectives* or simply *perspective* to our students. What does this word mean when

reading and writing fiction and nonfiction, looking at a photograph, or analyzing a primary source document? Why is this important to think about when reading? If your students are unfamiliar with this term or need to review, begin by brainstorming synonyms for the word *perspective* as this is a helpful way to engage your students in initial discussions. Creating a Word Web serves as a visual for synonyms of the word *perspective*. Synonyms may include: *attitude*, *viewpoint*, *position*, and *frame of reference*.

Please note that the word *opinion* has been deliberately omitted from the list, although students may offer it as a synonym for *perspective*. *Opinion* and *perspective* are two important words in the field of reading comprehension, and we concede that they are related. However, *opinion* can involve a quick judgment that's not necessarily based on fact, and we want students to see that *perspective* stems from the *way in which* someone views the world and that this view is steeped in a person's life experiences. In fact, you might consider engaging your students in a discussion about the differences between the words *perspective* and *opinion* in order to deepen their understanding. For example, using *Cinderella* as an example, the stepmother's *opinion* of Cinderella is that she is worthless because she is poor. This *opinion* is grounded in her *perspective* about life in a society that values money, royalty, and power and where these attributes are equivalent with worthiness and happiness.

We have found that the most helpful synonym for *perspective* is *lens*. As students encounter complex texts, they will look through different lenses to analyze texts for evidence of power, economic status, race, gender, religion, etc. (see Figure 3.2). As you continue to help students attain a deeper understanding of the word *perspective*, try using prompts that encourage them to identify their own perspectives about various topics. Ask, "How do you feel about the school serving soda in the lunchroom?" or "Do you think school should begin later in the morning?" Be sure to move students past their initial opinions about these issues by providing follow-up questions that lead them to identify their point of view. For example, a student may have the opinion that school should serve soda in the lunchroom. Once students have looked past their initial ideas, such as "Soda tastes good" or "I'd like to have it at school," they may begin to reveal their perspective, such as "Within my family, I've been raised to believe that everyone should have a choice." Noting the various feelings about an issue and the different positions taken can help students understand that each person has a perspective, and sometimes those perspectives conflict. Students will begin to see that there are many perspectives within a classroom, just as there are within texts.

TEACHING TIP

Lens is a helpful vocabulary word to use when teaching multiple perspectives. It reminds readers of the active work they need to do to see different points of view. It allows students to think critically about factors such as power, religion, gender, race, economic status, etc. Consider creating a chart like this Critical Lenses chart in order to remind students to use various lenses when examining texts.

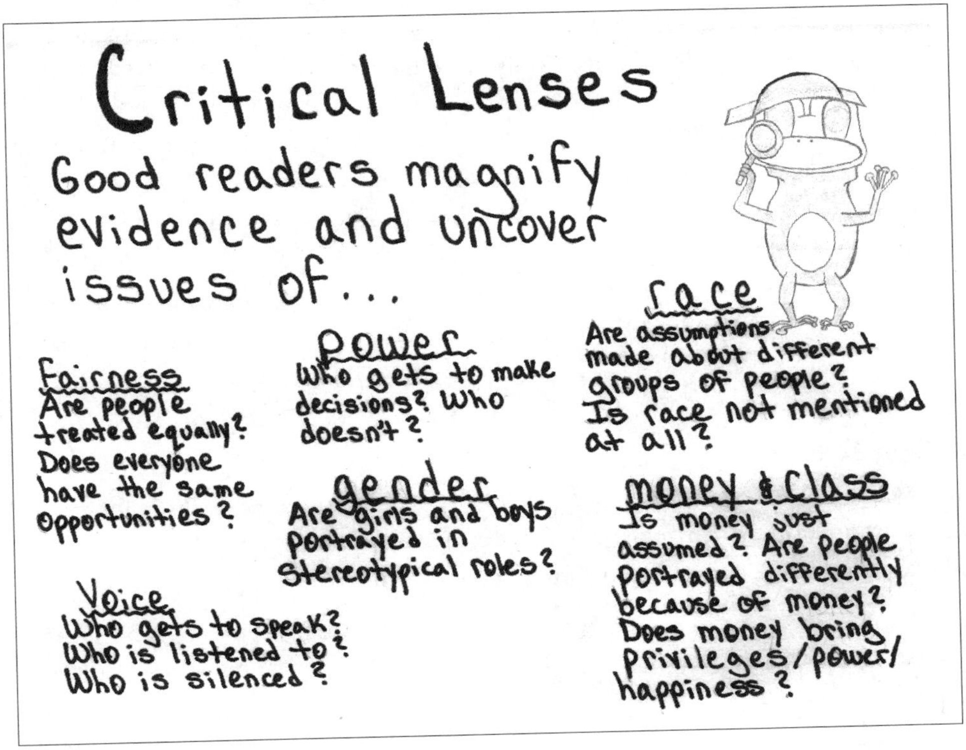

Figure 3.2 Critical Lenses Chart

Teaching Interpretation: Multiple Perspectives

Identifying Text Evidence

Students have learned how to generate initial claims, use graphic organizers or their readers' notebooks to collect and organize evidence, cite text correctly, and rank their evidence from weakest to strongest (see Chapters 1 and 2). Now students are ready to apply all of these skills and use text evidence to write strong literary responses.

First, students begin to collect text evidence by identifying the different characters and points of view in a text. We used "The Wrong Lunch Line" by Nicholasa Mohr as an example text for students to identify the various perspectives represented. Although this may seem like an easy task, as texts become more complex, students will be required not only to identify the perspectives of the main people (the named characters) but also groups of people (as named by the author and in society). These groups may be identified and labeled according to their religion, race, age, gender, or economic status, etc. However, it's important to lead students to consider that sometimes labels are wrong or used incorrectly; sometimes they are imposed on groups of people. Sometimes groups of people disagree, and there is conflict regarding their labels. Labels tend to overlook the intersection and overlapping identities experienced by many people and groups.

With this in mind, identifying multiple perspectives could be seen as a huge task. However, as we live in an increasingly diverse society, we believe schools and teachers have a responsibility to raise awareness of the views of others. This can be done by exposing students to the challenges and sensitivities surrounding complex issues. When asked to work cooperatively, students can apply such considerations during their discussions as they make lists of people and groups represented in "The Wrong Lunch Line." These lists can be created on sticky notes, in their reader's notebooks, or on chart paper.

Annotating Text

Learning how to annotate a text is important. It enables students to leave tracks of their thinking as they underline or circle parts of the text they think are important. Teach your students to annotate using a transcribed copy, photocopy, or personal copies of a text that

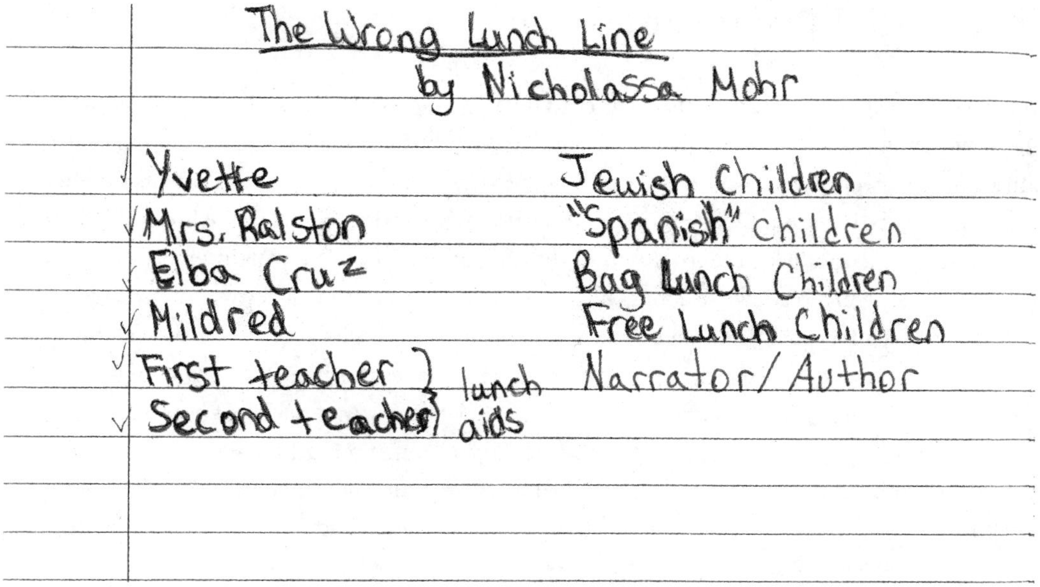

The Wrong Lunch Line
by Nicholassa Mohr

✓ Yvette	Jewish Children
✓ Mrs. Ralston	"Spanish" children
✓ Elba Cruz	Bag Lunch Children
✓ Mildred	Free Lunch Children
✓ First teacher } lunch	Narrator/Author
✓ Second teacher } aids	

Figure 3.3 Student Identifying Characters and Groups

students can write on. Be explicit when teaching your students to annotate, and remind them to look through onlyone or two lenses at a time and then build upon their lists. For example, students may first look for characters' names and then look for evidence of their perspective. Encourage students to always ask questions of the text and jot notes in the margins.

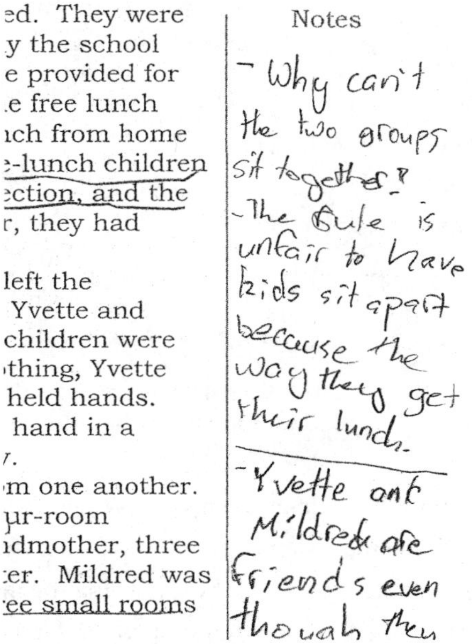

ed. They were
y the school
e provided for
e free lunch
ch from home
e-lunch children
ction, and the
r, they had

left the
Yvette and
children were
thing, Yvette
held hands.
hand in a
r.
m one another.
ur-room
dmother, three
er. Mildred was
ee small rooms

Notes

- Why can't the two groups sit together?
- The Rule is unfair to have kids sit apart because the way they get their lunch.

- Yvette and Mildred are friends even though they

Figure 3.4 Student Annotating Text

Inferential Comprehension

Interpretation stems from students' abilities to infer a person's feelings and motivations. Since identifying a character's perspective is an inferential reading comprehension task, we need to anticipate that we will have students in our classroom who need support. As students do the big work of locating multiple perspectives, teachers can provide support in the form of strategies, models, and practice time in order to help students who struggle with inferential comprehension. As students read, write about, and interpret the multiple perspectives found within complex texts, inferential thinking is required for deeper understanding and analytical thinking. Students need to ask themselves questions such as "How does this person or group of people feel?" "Why are they feeling that way?" In order to delve deeply into the challenge of identifying the multiple perspectives in a text, students must first activate their inferential reading skills and empathize with the people or groups portrayed in the text. It may be helpful to display inferential comprehension prompts (see the Teaching Tip box below). Students may refer to this list when they begin to notice whose perspective is revealed in the text.

TEACHING TIP

- Notice people's physical movements. How do these actions reveal the person's feelings?
- Notice what is said. How does the dialogue reflect the character's perspective and thinking?
- Notice decisions and choices. What does this reveal about the character's beliefs and positions?

Identifying the Characters' Feelings

After students identify the people and groups represented in the text, model how they can return to the text to find evidence that reveals the characters' feelings. Students can highlight or underline text evidence. We recommend that students are provided with or prompted to create a chart in their readers' notebooks to help them organize the evidence they are collecting.

Model this work by using the character Yvette from "The Wrong Lunch Line" in order to construct an interpretation about her feelings. Choosing the main character in a story is a useful teaching strategy because there is likely to be substantial text evidence to support students' theories about the character's feelings. This may provide multiple entry points for students to engage in discussion, writing, and overall participation.

First, you may want to begin by inviting students to view "The Wrong Lunch Line" through Yvette's eyes. Help them do this by asking the inferential thinking question, "How does Yvette feel?" After students have had time to think about Yvette's feelings, use the Interpretation Framework to guide your modeling of how to construct interpretations.

We find it helpful to use the Constructing an Interpretation chart to model this work. Here, the question "How does Yvette feel?" generates the ideas *confused*, *humiliated*, *sad*, and *embar-*

rassed. You may want to organize students' text evidence into categories such as "dialogue" and "actions," in order to show students what kinds of evidence they find to support their claims. In addition, you might use the "rethinking" part of the chart to examine ideas that could be more specific, such as "sad." For these words, encourage your students to rethink.

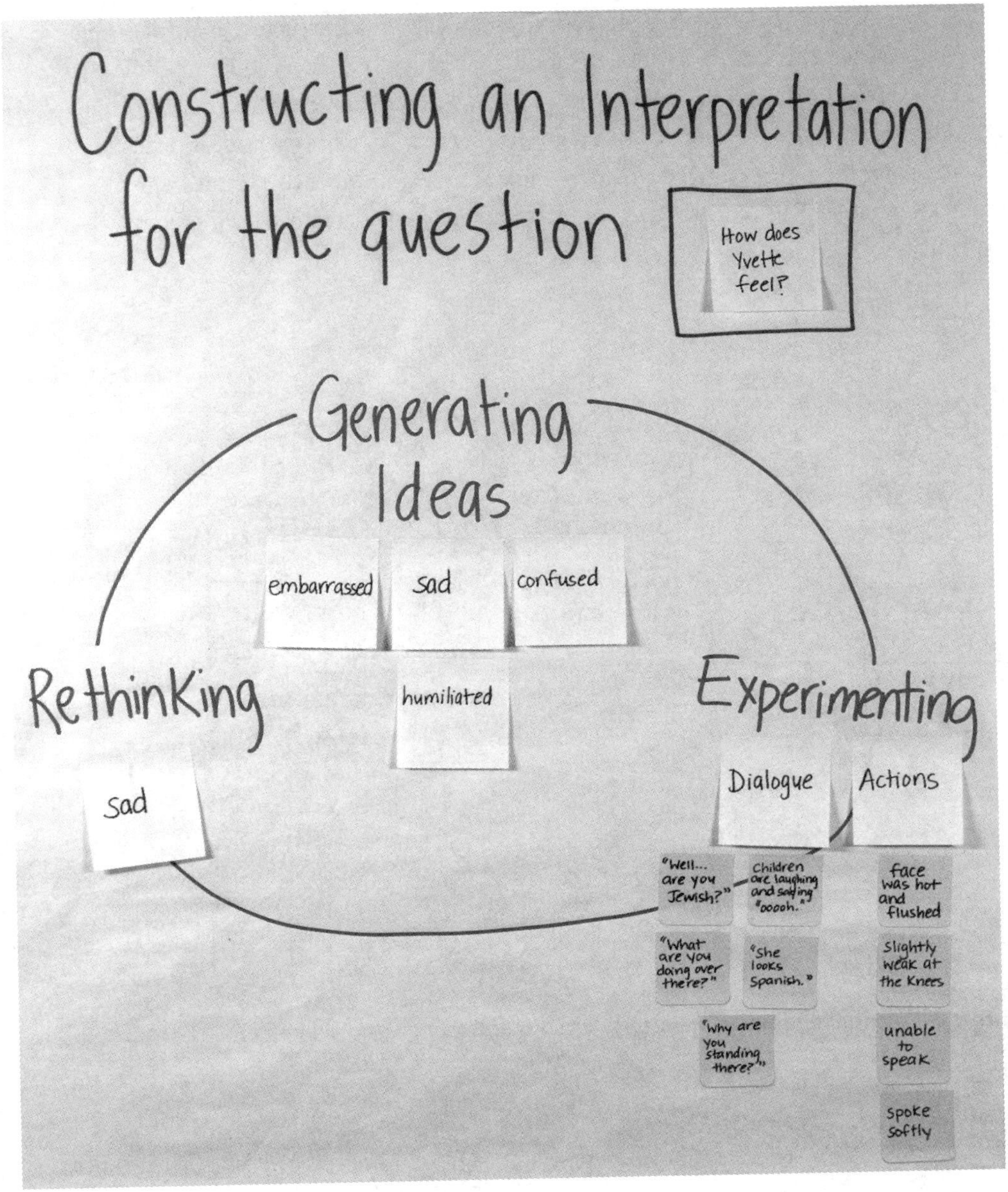

Figure 3.5 Interpretation Framework Chart

After working together to construct interpretations for Yvette's feelings, ask your students to continue gathering text evidence for all of the characters' feelings in the story. They can continue recording their ideas in their reader's notebooks (see Figure 3.6). You'll also find a blank template at the end of this chapter (see Figure 3.18).

After students have collected text evidence in their notebooks, you might consider bringing the class together for a discussion about their ideas and accompanying text evidence. We have found that an interactive chart is useful in guiding initial conversations about multiple characters' perspectives. First, post the event or scene, as well as the characters' names, in the circles on the chart (see Figure 3.7). Next, encourage your students to write their ideas on sticky notes and place them next to the characters' names (see Figure 3.8). This creates a great visual for elementary-aged students to compare and contrast characters' feelings and perspectives.

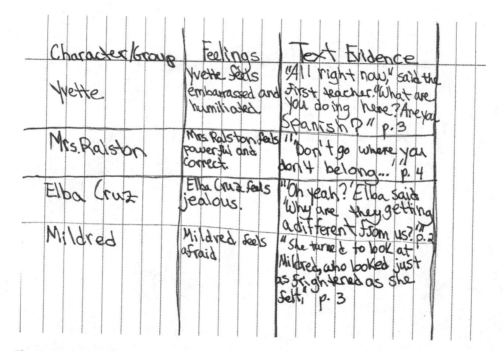

Figure 3.6 Student Identifying Characters' Feelings and Citing Text Evidence

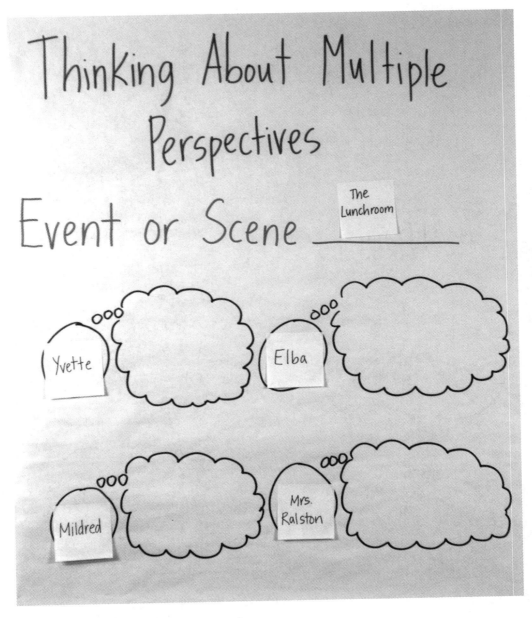

Figure 3.7 Multiple Perspectives Chart: Before

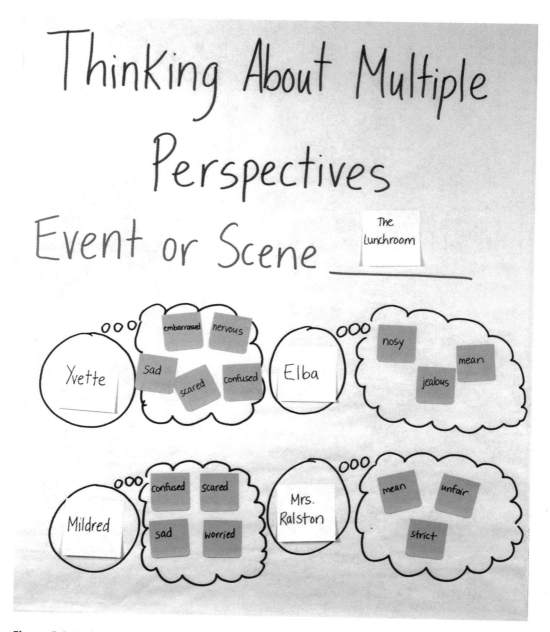

Figure 3.8 Multiple Perspectives Chart: After

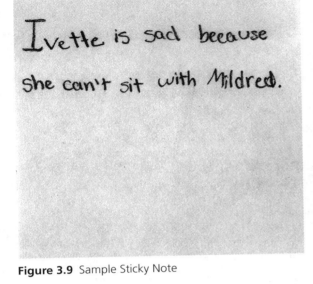

Ivette is sad because she can't sit with Mildred.

Figure 3.9 Sample Sticky Note

Strategically choose one of your students' responses as you continue to model. You may want to select a response that reflects inferential thinking, is representative of many of your students' responses, and can be used to demonstrate how to form and then strengthen an interpretation. For example, a common student response might be, "I think Yvette feels sad when the teacher yells at her." Ask, "Does anyone agree?" After hearing from a variety of students, ask them to return to the text to highlight or underline evidence that best supports the theory that Yvette feels sad.

Depending on the needs of your classroom, students can do this work independently, with a partner, or within small groups. Listen to the evidence that students offer. Encourage students to consider whether the evidence they've offered best supports the word *sad*. In this case, it is helpful to move students toward the process of *rethinking* their initial claims by asking, "After reviewing the text and finding this evidence, is it possible that our thinking is inaccurate? Are there other ideas from our peers that we can consider?" After giving students the opportunity to rethink either in small discussion groups or in their reader's notebooks, you might say, "It seems

that now we are making the claim that Yvette feels embarrassed and humiliated. I've noticed that many of you have supported this claim with strong evidence from the text." Remind students how to accurately cite text (RL.5.1, 6.1, 7.1, 8.1). After students have generated initial ideas and collected text evidence about the characters' feelings, they are ready to construct interpretations about the characters' perspectives.

Sample Lesson

When teaching multiple perspectives, we've found it helps to have our students look through the lenses of the characters, the author, and the world. The following lesson demonstrates the type of work you might ask students to do independently or in groups, using these three categories. As your students do this work, you want them to be actively engaged with the text. This may come in the form of students using sticky notes while they are reading, jotting notes in their readers' notebooks, or annotating a copy of the text.

LESSON
SNAPSHOT

Lesson Snapshot:
Multiple Perspectives

CCSS: RL.3.4, 4.4, 5.4, 6.4, 7.4, 8.4

Teaching Objectives:

- Students will identify and analyze multiple perspectives.
- Students will support their claims with relevant text evidence.
- Students will construct interpretations about the perspectives of characters and authors.

Materials:

- Select a text that contains a variety of characters' perspectives or choose from the Text Recs list.
- Select or create a graphic organizer that complements the text.

Steps:

1. Decide if students will work in small groups, pairs, or independently.
2. Model with the whole class how to interpret the perspective of a character or the author by asking, "What does _____ believe?" and "Why does this character or author have this point of view?"
3. Have students look back at their text evidence to support their claims.
4. Have students try this work on their own or in small groups.
5. Ask students to consider how the perspectives of the characters and the author helps us to construct interpretations about the world.

(To differentiate instruction, refer to the Novice and Advanced Readers suggestions located toward the end of this chapter.)

Constructing Interpretations About Characters' Perspectives

Now that students have identified Yvette's feelings and found the strongest text evidence to support their ideas, they are able to begin constructing an interpretation of Yvette's perspective in "The Wrong Lunch Line." This can be done independently with students responding in their reader's notebooks, or this can be done cooperatively during small-group discussions. To do this, guide your students with the following prompt: "What does Yvette believe?" This type of question can create a space for students to contribute several ideas. At the same time, it can help with those who are grappling with moving beyond the characters' feelings toward constructing an interpretation about Yvette's perspective.

Provide follow-up prompts and questions when needed such as, "What does Yvette think is fair?" "How does she think she should live her life?" Students can continue with this iterative process to reveal the perspectives of other characters and groups in the story. Ask students to compare and contrast these perspectives using their critical lenses, noting similarities and differences. Ask students to consider the following: "Why might these characters/groups have this particular point of view?" "Why might these characters/groups have conflicting points of view?" and "What might be obscured and why?" Further discussions may center around whether or not the characters or groups represented in the text are static or dynamic, whether they have fixed or shifting perspectives. Remind students to ground their thinking in the details provided by the text as they develop their theories about other characters and groups (RL.4.6, 5.6). See Figure 3.10.

All readers bring themselves to a text. Whichever text you are using, key questions to consider include: "What do I think about the character's perspective?" "What connections and experiences do I share with these characters?" "How does my perspective affect my interpretation?" As we help our students ferret out their ideas to revise and hone their interpretations of a text, we want them to be cognizant of how their perspectives shape their interpretations. Students will recognize that their interpretations of characters may differ from those of their peers, based on each student's experiences, beliefs, and backgrounds. The goal is to blend these ideas so that students aren't just responding to what they think, but they are still drawing heavily from the text and finding evidence that supports their thinking. It is important that students continue to share, question, and revise their interpretations during this circular-thinking process. Students will challenge their thinking by applying their interpretations to different forms of discussions and writing (RL5.3, 6.3, 7.3, 8.3).

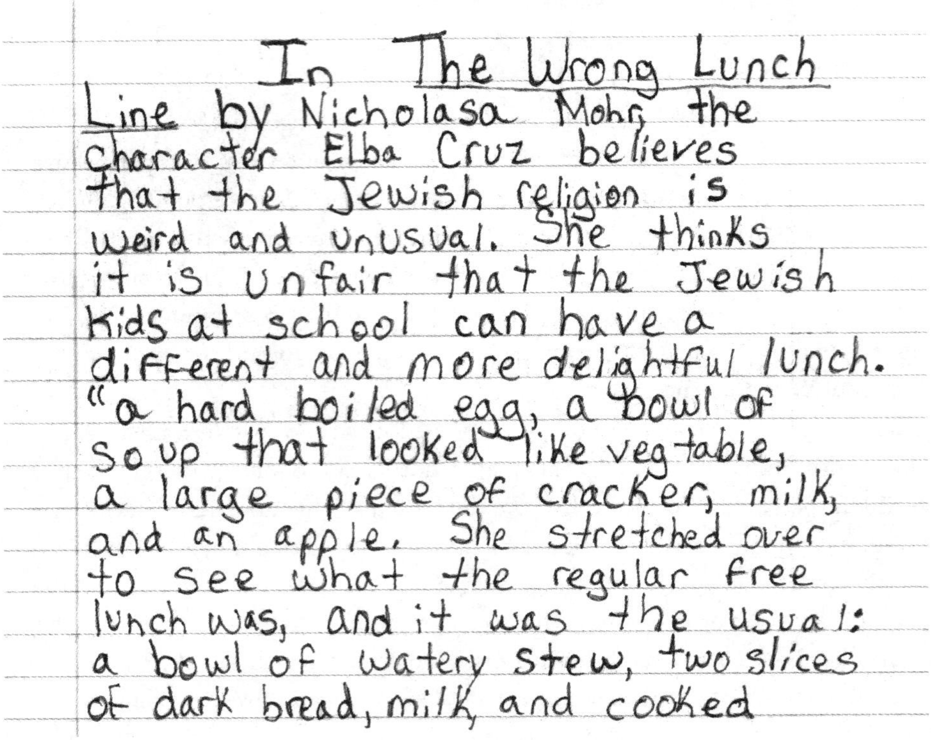

> In *The Wrong Lunch Line* by Nicholasa Mohr, the character Elba Cruz believes that the Jewish religion is weird and unusual. She thinks it is unfair that the Jewish kids at school can have a different and more delightful lunch. "a hard boiled egg, a bowl of soup that looked like vegtable, a large piece of cracker, milk, and an apple. She stretched over to see what the regular free lunch was, and it was the usual: a bowl of watery stew, two slices of dark bread, milk, and cooked

Figure 3.10 Student Thinking About a Character's Perspective

Hot Seat

You may want to engage your students in an activity called Hot Seat. We learned this activity from a beloved English teacher who taught for more than twenty-five years and who was known for her ability to bring texts to life. For this activity, students decide which character in a text they would most like to question. For example, students may choose Yvette from "The Wrong Lunch Line." Ask students to imagine that Yvette is coming to the classroom. They are going to ask her questions that may help sharpen their understanding of her point of view. This critical-thinking work is significant because students not only have to form questions, but they must also answer the questions based on a combination of their inferences, interpretations, and evidence from the text.

Students can write their questions in their reader's notebooks. Be on the lookout for students who are continuing to rely solely on their inferencing skills rather than on thinking about questions that could reveal a hidden idea that has not been previously considered. For example, if a student asks Yvette, "How did you *feel* when the lunchroom monitor told you that you could not sit with Mildred?" or "Were you *afraid* when you had to go see the assistant principal, Mrs. Ralston?" redirect your students to consider questions that could reveal what the character might *think*, instead of *feel*. Examples of questions students might write in order to stretch beyond their inferencing skills include:

- Why did you think it would be OK to sit with Mildred?
- What do you think about how the kids are seated in the lunchroom?
- Why did you say that Mrs. Ralston is dumb?

Choose a student to be in the "hot seat." This student will assume the role of the character and do her or his best to answer the questions generated by the class (see Figure 3.11). Be sure to select a student who has been a close reader of the text and can base her or his answers on what the character might actually say. In short, you are looking for a student who can effectively step into the shoes of the character. The other students can take turns asking questions, and they can write down the character's responses in their reader's notebooks. This process may continue for as many questions as time permits.

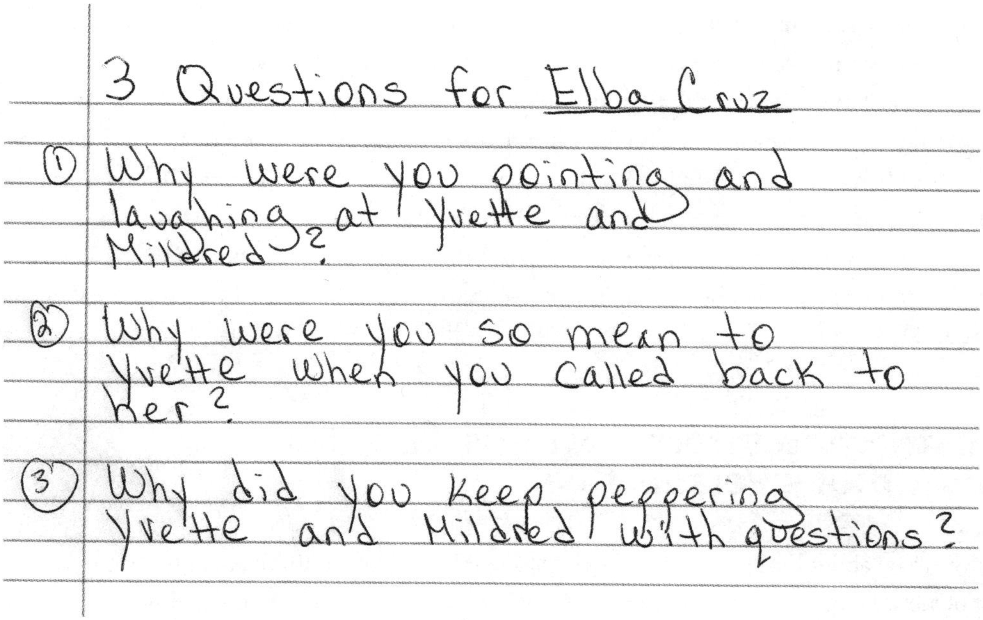

3 Questions for Elba Cruz

① Why were you pointing and laughing at Yvette and Mildred?

② Why were you so mean to Yvette when you called back to her?

③ Why did you keep peppering Yvette and Mildred with questions?

Figure 3.11 Sample "Hot Seat" Questions

Afterward, the class can engage in a discussion about how hearing directly from the character has helped students gain some new insights and better understand the characters' point of view. Summarize conversations you hear between students, and name the work the students are doing during their discussions.

Students may focus on why Yvette took a certain action—for example, the reasons why Yvette went on the lunch line with Mildred. This can help students think about Yvette's true motivation and uncover themes within the text (see Chapter 5). Other students may think about characters as complex people whose motivations are not always clear. Why did the assistant principal and the lunch monitors insist on organizing groups of students this way in the story? Was it just, as some readers might say, "to keep kids apart," or are there other factors involved? This kind of thinking can help students consider who has control, or power, and how that power is used. Subsequently, the activity "hot seat" can help students think about some of the big ideas the author may want them to consider as readers.

Writing From a Character's Perspective

As a culminating writing assignment, ask students to write a first-person vignette—as if they are one of the characters from the text. This could be done as a "Dear Diary" entry or a journal entry. This type of writing helps students peel away layers of meaning by revealing a character's inner thoughts. You can also invite students to challenge a character's actions. For example, students could write a letter to Mrs. Ralston expressing Yvette's point of view and arguing why she should be allowed to sit with Mildred. In short, you are inviting students to ask themselves: "If given the chance to speak, what might other characters say?" How might our understanding of the story change if it were told from Mildred's point of view? Or Elba Cruz's? Or one of the lunch monitor's? Students can "retell" a part of the story through the eyes of another character and determine whether this account would mirror Yvette's, or if it would differ, and what can be learned from this point of view. Use an interactive chart to scaffold the writing assignment (see Figure 3.12).

Constructing Interpretations About the Author's Perspective

After thinking about the characters' perspectives, guide students to think about the author's point of view. Finding the author's perspective will enhance students' understanding of the purpose of the text and strengthen their interpretations.

Locating the Author's Perspective Through Setting

To begin, you may want to remind students that everything an author does is purposeful. Ask students, "How is the author's perspective revealed in this text?" One way to start uncovering this is to invite students to think about how the author's perspective is influenced by the time period and setting. "The Wrong Lunch Line," for example, takes place at the end of World War II in the United States. You might ask students:

"Why did the author choose this time period?"

"What was going on during this time period?"

"What was the mood?" (see Chapter 2)

"How does the author use the mood of the time period to develop the tone of the text?" (see Chapter 2)

"What does this reveal about the author's perspective?"

Locating the Author's Perspective Through Main Characters

Readers may discover that the author's point of view is sometimes conveyed through the perspective of the main character. For example, in "The Wrong Lunch Line," students may think that Yvette's perspective reveals the author's point of view. Students may say, "The author believes that everyone should sit together." Often, students' interpretations of the author's perspective can be one-dimensional, referring only to one character's reactions, decisions, and stance. As you challenge your students to generate new ideas, experiment, and rethink their interpretations, while considering the many perspectives of the characters, students will construct rich interpretations that reveal the complex perspective of the author. After prompting students to consider all the characters' perspectives, students may begin to see that the author's point of view is revealed through a combination of characters: Yvette's, Mildred's, Elba's, and Mrs. Ralston's. As our students become more sophisticated readers, they may discover that characters who create conflict also reveal the author's perspective. Students may rethink their original claim, ultimately noting that, "The author believes that everyone should sit together, no matter their race, religion, or how much money they have." As students rethink their claims, encourage them to find text evidence that supports their ideas.

Thinking Critically About the Author's Perspective

Next, challenge your students to consider *why* the author felt his or her perspective was important to share through the text. What themes emerge based on the author's point of view? Teachers may want to refer to the Critical Lenses chart (see Figure 3.2) in order to support students' growth in making these connections. For example, you might ask,

"What is the author's perspective about the type of place school can be sometimes?" (RL.6.6, 7.6, 8.6). From this starting point, students may talk about issues of power, race, religion, and age.

Readers may come to the conclusion that the lenses they are reading with also reveal themes that are part of the author's point of view. Students may rethink their original interpretations and experiment with new ideas, combining their thoughts to form rich interpretations. For example, "The author reveals her perspective through the eyes of Yvette and Mildred, believing that schools can be a place that reflect issues of fairness and power, issues that exist in our everyday lives." This claim demonstrates how students delved deeply into the text and used the Interpretation Framework to construct an interpretation that illuminates the author's perspective and main message.

Constructing Interpretations About the World

Invite students to continue to use their critical lenses to develop theories about the world based on the reading. Ask, "How do the experiences of the characters/groups, along with our understanding of the author's perspective, help us construct interpretations about the world?" For example, a close reading and multiple discussions of "The Wrong Lunch Line" may bring to light ways in which schools, like Yvette's and Mildred's, can be perceived as divisive places that separate groups of people, rather than collaborative environments that bring people together. Evidence to support this claim can be found by reviewing the text and listing the ways in which the students are separated. Your students may create a list that includes race, religion, economic status, and grade level. Later, when asked to respond to these ideas, students may extend this list based on observations of how children are separated in their own school, including by groups such as gender and popularity.

A further analysis of the list of people/groups that students created during their initial work on multiple perspectives might lead your students to interpret this text as one that illuminates conflict between two main groups, for example: children and adults. Based on evidence collected from the text, ask students to consider which ideas might "school" symbolize. For example, students might determine that "school," in this text, symbolizes an institution or a system of rules imposed upon those without power or a say in things. As a result of reading, reflecting on, and discussing any text, encourage students to ask themselves, "What interpretations can I construct about the world?" Using the Critical Lenses chart (see Figure 3.2), students may begin by brainstorming and then creating definitions of the themes that have emerged in the reading. For example, using our model text, "The Wrong Lunch Line," students can use their critical lenses to take part in small- or whole-group conversations to generate the following list of themes in this text: injustice, discrimination, rich versus poor, equality, power, fairness, and racism. Create a class chart so that all students can share and have access to the ideas generated. From this list, ask students to choose the theme that resonates most strongly with them as a result of reading and discussing the text. Ask students to consider, "What do these themes mean to me?" and "How does this theme exist in the world and connect to my own life?" Remind students that themes are universal, which means they exist beyond the confines of the pages of a text. (RL.5.2, 6.2, 7.2, 8.2). This work can be done with any text you choose.

Looking Across Texts

For elementary-aged readers who feel uncertain about how to find the perspectives in the text, assure them that they've actually done this work before. Use what is familiar and comfortable and challenge them to apply what they know to what is unfamiliar. For example, when talking about perspective and multiple attitudes, use books like *The True Story of the Three Little Pigs* or *The Stinky Cheese Man and Other Stupid Fairy Tales,* both by Jon Scieszka and Lane Smith. The story of the *Three Little Pigs* and other tales may be familiar to novice readers from their early childhood. Begin by making a list of the people or groups represented in the text, and challenge your readers to push their thinking further and ask questions such as, "Who is telling this story?" "How does their perspective affect my understanding of this story?" and "If someone else told this story, how might it change?" Here is an example of an interactive chart you might create (see Figure 3.12), as well as a student's response to the question, "What is the wolf's perspective?" in *The True Story of the Three Little Pigs* (see Figure 3.13).

Ask readers who have mastered locating the perspectives represented in a text to think about the perspectives *not* represented in the text. Ask students to consider, "Who is left out?" "Who has remained silent?" Students will call upon their inferential reading skills and think about people or groups of people who are silenced or not represented. Ask students to create a list of these people or groups, and encourage them to discuss why they think the author chose to leave these perspectives out of the text. Ask questions such as "Why is this perspective left out?" and "What would happen if this person's or group's voice was present in the text?"

Figure 3.12 New Angle Chart

For readers who are now able to identify the various perspectives of characters in texts, challenge them to think deeply about the perspective of the author and what he or she attempts to convey. For example, Chris Van Allsburg often writes about issues in society, and his books encourage readers to grapple with these issues. In *The Wretched Stone*, Van Allsburg's writing can be interpreted as a commentary on modern-day society, and students can be challenged to think about what Van Allsburg's point of view is. "What does Van Allsburg fear may happen with our continued fascination and insatiability with technology?" In *The Widow's Broom*, challenge readers to consider what Van Allsburg seems to be saying about how people sometimes treat one another. "Which people in our society could be represented by the broom? How have they been treated? Do they continue to be treated this way today?"

Name: _Ben_
Three Little Pigs

1. What is the wolf's perspective?

The wolf's perspective is that he didn't choose to
hurt the pigs. All he wanted was a cup of sugar, but
no one would give it to him. He was framed and he
feels acused. The pigs were being mean so he was feeling
bullied.

Figure 3.13 Ben's Response

The Interpretation Framework Process

GENERATING IDEAS: Students are working to read the text with their minds open to thinking about the characters' feelings. As they marinate in the ideas presented to them, students are encouraged to walk in the characters' shoes so they may think about the characters' feelings and identify their perspectives, as well as the author's point of view. Students may need additional support from teachers or peers and can benefit from considering the following questions: "Who is the narrator? Who are the people or groups involved? What are the perspectives of those people or groups in the text? How do the characters' actions reveal their perspectives? How do their decisions/choices reveal their perspectives?"

RETHINKING: As students create initial interpretations it is important for them to consider alternate ideas posed by their peers. Students will grapple over keywords and phrases that might reveal the perspective of the characters and the author, and then use this evidence to revise their thinking. To help students consider alternate theories, encourage them to read the Author's Note in longer texts, to look for recurring ideas and themes across a text, and to consider not only the words but also the actions of the characters. It is also important for students to think about the differences between *opinion* and *perspective* when revising their claims.

EXPERIMENTING: When students have a claim about the perspectives of the characters and the author, they need to find the strongest text evidence. Students will then weigh which evidence best supports their ideas as they construct an interpretation. They should also think about how this evidence relates to the world, which evidence is missing, which characters are silenced, and which evidence best relates to their own life experiences.

Strategies for Novice Readers

Drawing upon students' visual learning styles is one way to help novice readers think about multiple perspectives. The picture book *Zoo*, written and illustrated by Anthony Browne, is a rich tool to use for this purpose. We recommend covering up the text so that students can examine the illustrations and note what Browne has chosen to make salient and why. For example, to help elementary-aged students begin to make inferences about how the characters feel, encourage them to notice the attention Browne gives to the size, facial expressions, and gestures of both people and animals. This can lead students to construct interpretations about the variety of perspectives in this text, including the author's perspective. After our fourth-grade students viewed the illustrations in *Zoo*, we gave them sticky notes and asked them to write down their observations. The students then displayed their sticky notes on large pieces of chart paper so they could share their ideas with their peers.

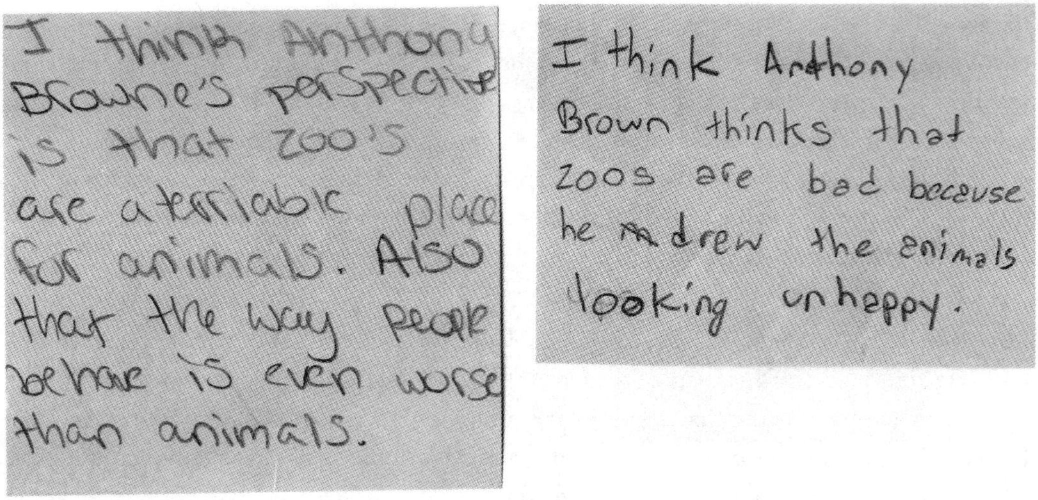

I think Anthony Browne's perspective is that zoo's are a terriable place for animals. Also that the way people behave is even worse than animals.

I think Anthony Brown thinks that zoos are bad because he drew the animals looking unhappy.

Figure 3.14 Interpreting the Author's Perspective

If . . . Try . . .

HELPING NOVICE READERS CREATE INTERPRETATIONS ABOUT MULTIPLE PERSPECTIVES

If . . .	Try . . .
Students are inferring . . . (You can tell because they are noticing only the characters' feelings, not their perspectives.)	Help students go deeper by saying, "Yes, but why does the character feel that way?" OR "What does the author want us to notice?"
Students are not identifying multiple perspectives . . . (You can tell because they are identifying only one point of view.)	First, go back to inferences and have students think about the many feelings the characters may be experiencing. What do these feelings reveal about their perspectives? From that starting point, guide them to think about why it is important to think about all of the characters' perspectives. Encourage students to "try on" different lenses. Refer to the Critical Lenses chart (see Figure 3.2).
Students are struggling to form a claim . . . (You can tell because they may be summarizing the text, gathering evidence that is unconnected, or they are stuck in the gray.)	You might begin by talking to students about what a claim is. Prompt them with questions such as "What do we learn from the characters' perspectives?" OR "What does the author want us to learn?" If your students are debating their idea and are stuck in the gray, great! Praise them for not seeing an issue as "black or white." Have them identify the questions they are grappling with. From there, a claim may emerge. Review sample claims from other texts you've used in the past and do some inquiry work. What makes this a claim? How did we make this claim?
Students are having difficulty identifying the author's point of view and connection to the world . . .	Prompt students with questions such as, "What is the author trying to teach you?" "Why did the author make this choice?" "What ideas about life does this text help us to think about?"

Figure 3.15 If . . . Try . . .

Strategies for Advanced Readers

For advanced readers who are able to interpret the perspectives of characters presented in fiction, challenge them to transfer the skills they've used to interpreting perspectives presented in nonfiction. We've found that many of our students tend to take in and accept all nonfiction as fact, rather than as angled writing that stems from the author's point of view. When students are asked to read nonfiction and examine the evidence presented, encourage them to consider the sources drawn upon to create the writing, the perspectives included, and the points of view that have been silenced and why (see Figure 3.16).

Teachers can consider the following three questions when teaching students to interpret multiple perspectives using nonfiction:

- Have I provided or taught students to look for a variety of primary source materials including speeches, photographs, advertisements, articles, etc., that reflect differing views on an event?
- Are these sources representative of groups who have been traditionally marginalized and ignored based on race, religion, gender, economic status, etc., rather than representative of primarily dominant groups?
- Have students been asked to mull over the ways in which different people/groups may perceive the same issue or event differently, and have students been encouraged to ask why?

Topic: Killer Whales in Captivity   Source(s): Captive Killer Whale Debate Video / WESH 2 News broadcast

Person/Group	Perspective	Text Evidence
Paul Spawn Psychologist	Believes its wrong to keep Killer Whales in captivity. Killer Whales in captivity behave differently then how they do in the wild.	"When you watch these poor animals performing these circus tricks in these tanks you have to shake your head and walk away from it."
John Ford Aquarium Care Taker	Believes it's OK to keep Killer Whales in Captivity.	"It makes an emotional bond that is unobtainable in other ways. Once people have seen a Killer Whale it may effect the way that they think about Killer whales."

Figure 3.16 Sample of an Advanced Reader's Graphic Organizer

The digital bin contains examples of the types of resources we want our students to have access to when considering multiple perspectives.

digitalbins.wordpress
.com/multiple
-perspectives

Taking a critical literacy approach in order to help students form interpretations, particularly regarding historical events and when examining primary source documents, can help bring validity to traditionally one-sided narratives and points of view. While there is not one way to define critical literacy, a commitment to social justice is foundational. Lewison, Flint, and Van Sluys (2002) synthesize theorists' interpretations of critical literacy into four interrelated, undergirding tenets: "(1) disrupting the commonplace, (2) interrogating multiple viewpoints, (3) focusing on sociopolitical issues, and (4) taking action and promoting social justice" (p. 382). Disrupting the commonplace involves seeing the "everyday through new lenses" (p. 383) in an attempt to disrupt the status quo. Interrogating multiple viewpoints includes considering the perspectives and views of others and "paying attention to and seeking out the voices of those who have been silenced or marginalized" (p. 383). Focusing on sociopolitical issues encourages challenging unequal power relationships, such as those influenced by gender, race, and class. Social action involves the work of thinking about what can be done to promote change. As societies become increasingly more diverse, students will need to become adept at puzzling over the many perspectives of an event or issue, which may sometimes conflict, in order to piece together a more accurate and socially just interpretation.

TEACHING TIP

Many students tend to take in and accept all nonfiction as fact. Help students understand that nonfiction writing is angled and that writers of nonfiction write from their point of view.

If . . . Try . . .

HELPING ADVANCED READERS CREATE INTERPRETATIONS ABOUT MULTIPLE PERSPECTIVES

If . . .	Try . . .
Students are finding lots of good evidence but not weighing it . . .	Discuss the purpose of finding strong text evidence. What does the evidence do? Students might want to do some inquiry work with sample evidence from their work with a previous text in order to review how the strongest evidence proved their claim. You want to encourage students to rank order their evidence and debate each piece. What are the pros and cons for using this piece of evidence when trying to prove their claim?
Students are making claims that are strong but could be even stronger . . .	Encourage students to make connections between the perspectives of the characters, the author's point of view, and what they are learning about life and the world.
Students are forming a strong claim and finding strong evidence but not rethinking . . .	You might begin by modeling the process of rethinking. You could say, "Even though you have a strong claim and strong evidence, it is important to always look for different angles. Try a different viewpoint and see how that affects your claim."
Students are critical readers but continue to examine the text through only one lens . . .	Use the Critical Lenses chart and encourage students to "try on" different lenses. How do they view the characters' perspectives through these different lenses?

Figure 3.17 If . . . Try . . .

Planning A Year of Teaching Multiple Perspectives

You may choose to teach multiple perspectives across the school year. If so, the following calendar can guide you. You may find, however, that your schedule does not allow for all of these suggestions. In that case, pick and choose which of these best suit your needs.

Multiple Perspectives Across the School Year

September: "What is perspective?" Use read-alouds or a class text to discuss the characters' points of view. Compare and contrast.

October: Focus your study on identifying the characters' perspectives—both those that are heard and those that are not heard. Have students identify text evidence to support their claims.

November: This month, highlight the author's perspective and have students discuss and debate their interpretations.

December: Connect your study of the characters' perspectives to our world today. How do their perspectives reflect people's perspectives in our world?

January: Use nonfiction, such as speeches or primary source documents, to analyze for multiple perspectives. Discuss the author's intent and connection to the world today.

February: Students should be able to identify multiple perspectives in texts and make initial claims about what the characters' perspectives show, why the author has created the characters' points of view, and how multiple perspectives enhance a reader's interpretation of the text.

March: This month, hone your students' ability to locate text evidence. Make sure they are selecting their evidence thoughtfully by weighing and comparing its strength. Also review how to cite sources and page numbers correctly.

April: Focus on students' ability to journey through the Interpretation Framework on their own. Can they generate ideas about multiple perspectives, experiment with evidence, and rethink their claims?

May: As your students locate multiple perspectives in texts, differentiate your instruction to help both your novice and advanced readers think more deeply by using the suggestions in the If . . . Try . . . boxes.

June: End your year of teaching multiple perspectives with a review of the Interpretation Framework process.

Character	Feelings	Text Evidence

Figure 3.18 Identifying Characters' Feelings

Character	Perspective	Text Evidence

Figure 3.19 Identifying Characters' Perspectives

Symbolism

*Reading Signs
and Symbols*

"When is a seed just a seed?"

In mid-February, *Dana's students were all seated in a group in front of her, their pencils and clipboards poised and ready for a quick reading assessment. Dana felt proud of the work her students had done constructing interpretations and gathering text evidence to support their claims. She was eager to plan next steps. As she read* The Lotus Seed *by Sherry Garland, she asked her students questions about the work they had done so far: making interpretations about multiple perspectives, mood, and figurative language. She read the beginning pages and then paused after reading this passage:*

> *She hid the seed*
> *in a special place*
> *under the family altar,*
> *wrapped in a piece of silk*
> *from the ao dai*
> *she wore that day.*
> *Whenever she felt sad*
> *or lonely,*
> *she took out the seed*
> *and thought of the*
> *brave young emperor.*

She then asked, "What might the lotus seed symbolize?" As her students' pencils flew over their papers, confident in their answers, eyes scanning and searching the text, Dana felt relieved and excited. She knew they must have rich ideas about what the lotus seed symbolized. Just then, one of her students, Nina, said, "This is easy. It says it right here. Do I just write down exactly what the text says?" A shock of alarm went through Dana. Did the other students also think the text stated outright what the seed symbolized? Were they confused about the word symbolize? Did they understand that they needed to make their own interpretations? "Write down what you believe the seed might symbolize," Dana answered Nina.

Later, as Dana read her students' responses, her worries were confirmed. "The seed symbolizes the emperor," Nina had written.

Dana shook her head, concerned that others may have written similar responses. "The seed symbolizes the emperor's garden," another student had written. Not only were their answers underdeveloped, but they provided no text evidence to support their claims. As Dana thought about their answers, she realized that her students hadn't made any inferences or interpretations. In fact, they hadn't even considered the seed itself and the symbolism inherent in a seed. They had gone straight to the text in search of answers without doing any original thinking, making connections, or generating their own ideas. Dana realized that she had two challenges. First, she needed to make sure her students understood what symbolism was and how it related to making interpretations. Second, she wanted to provide her students with some new, more sophisticated strategies for finding and using text evidence to support their interpretations.

What does the lotus seed *symbolize*? Use text evidence.

The lotus symbolizes the emperor.

Figure 4.1 Nina's Pre-Assessment

Rationale and Common Core State Standards Connection

The Common Core standards require students beginning in sixth grade to find the meaning of figurative language (RL.6.4, 7.4, 8.4). Figurative language (see Chapter 1) includes the study of metaphors, similes, and symbols in a text. These elements require students to read a text closely to notice how something like a rock or a bird might signal ideas that are not stated outright in the text. For many students, learning to read closely in order to look at a rock or a bird differently is challenging and unappealing. They ask questions like, "Why do we need to learn how to do this? What's the point?" or "Do I need to look for symbols in every book? In every text? All the time?" or "If the teacher doesn't tell me the bird is a symbol, how would I know?" These questions are all too familiar in classrooms. Students may look at this type of reading work as tedious and unimportant.

Of course we understand our students' frustrations. As adults, we may think back on our own experiences in middle school and high school, trying to read poetry and various complex texts with a lens for symbolism, only to feel frustrated and angry at ourselves when we couldn't find any or didn't drive our thinking *deep enough*. Our resentment toward poetry and texts only grew as a few precocious students pointed out symbols that seemed to be chosen at random. We wondered to ourselves, "How did they do that?" "How did they know that was a symbol?" "Where in the text does it reveal this information?" Fortunately, the work of locating symbols can be taught concretely using strategies. By using the Interpretation Framework, the process of interpreting symbols can be accessible to students.

Getting Ready

Pre-Assessment

Use the pre-assessment tool to identify your students' prior knowledge about symbols. You may want to use a picture book, a poem, an excerpt from a text, or a multimedia tool. This is an important first step, as students' understanding of symbolism may vary from the concrete (logos, national or school symbols) to the abstract (weather, animals, colors), and ultimately to metaphors and allusions (biblical figures, text-to-text references, relationships, etc.).

digitalbins.wordpress
.com/symbolism

Choose a text of your choice or select one from the Text Recs list. Locate an object, animal, color, food, or name from the text, and ask your students the questions below. Just like the pre-assessment you may have created for Chapters 1, 2, and 3, you can read the text aloud to your students or transcribe it so they can read it silently. Use the following questions in order to assess your students' understanding of identifying symbols and interpreting symbolism:

For example, if you have chosen the picture book *The Patchwork Quilt* by Valerie Flournoy, you might ask, "What does the quilt symbolize? Why did the author create this symbol?" If you have chosen to use an excerpt from a chapter book, make sure your students are familiar with the story, as it will be difficult for them to discuss symbolism without having a fuller understanding of the text. Using poetry is a terrific way to assess students' understanding of symbolism. We have also provided a list of possible symbols that you might want to look for in a text when creating your pre-assessment (see Figure 4.2). We have categorized these symbols into three groups to help you differentiate your assessment based on the needs and ages of your students.

1. What does the _____ symbolize in the text? Use text evidence to support your answer.

2. Can you find a symbol on this page/in this scene? What does it symbolize?

3. Why does the author create the symbol, _____?

Common Symbols	Common Literary Symbols		Challenging Literary Symbols
Logos	Animals	Seasons	Idioms, Fairy Tales, Legends, etc.
Buildings and Structures	Weather	Shapes	Biblical Allusions
National Symbols, Monuments	Objects	Light/Dark	Juxtaposition of Settings
School Symbols	Colors	Nature	Passage of Time
Signs	Setting	Food	Relationships, Power
Math, Science, Technology	Names	Numbers	Actions

Figure 4.2 Literary Symbols

Text Recs: Dana and Sonja's Book Bins

We love using the following texts in our classrooms when teaching symbolism:

Picture Books	Chapter Books	Nonfiction, Short Stories, Poems
The Patchwork Quilt by Valerie Flournoy	Rickshaw Girl by Mitali Perkins	"The Bats" by Alma Flor Ada
The Keeping Quilt by Patricia Polacco	Frindle by Andrew Clements	"My Grandmother's Hair" by Cynthia Rylant
The Bracelet by Yoshiko Uchida	Tiger Rising by Kate DiCamillo	"Los Pelitos" by Sandra Cisneros
The Granddaughter Necklace by Sharon Dennis Wyeth	Sylvia & Aki by Winifred Conkling	"Thank you, Ma'am" by Langston Hughes
The Lotus Seed by Sherry Garland	Number the Stars by Lois Lowry	"Eleven" by Sandra Cisneros
Each Kindness & The Other Side by Jacqueline Woodson	Julie of the Wolves by Jean Craighead George	"The Great Colossus" by Emma Lazarus
The Wretched Stone and The Widow's Broom by Chris Van Allsburg	Where the Mountain Meets the Moon by Grace Lin	"The Necklace" by Guy de Maupassant
Wangari's Trees of Peace: A True Story from Africa by Jeanette Winter	Esperanza Rising by Pam Muñoz Ryan	"The Road Not Taken" by Robert Frost
A Place Where Sunflowers Grow by Amy Lee-Tai	Bloomability by Sharon Creech	"Firework" by Katy Perry
	Tuck Everlasting by Natalie Babbitt	"Here Comes the Sun" by the Beatles
	The Giver by Lois Lowry	"The Monkey's Paw" by W. W. Jacobs
		"Early Autumn" by Langston Hughes

Figure 4.3 Text Recs

Launching

"What Are Symbols?"

A discussion about common symbols is a great way to launch a study on symbolism. We find that most students can easily articulate which brand a logo represents, including a sophisticated un-

derstanding of the logo's intent—often a homage to the excellent work of the advertisers! For example, when students see the Nike logo, they immediately state the brand name and motto, and they can easily describe the feelings and emotions evoked by the logo. This work segues easily to a conversation about the purpose of symbols in our environment, daily lives, and the study of literature.

Symbols are important in our everyday lives because they can be filled with meaning. They are powerful because they can send messages, evoke feelings, and trigger memories. Just like superheroes with secret identities, symbols lie in wait, seemingly unimportant, full of mystery and deeper meaning. Although at first students may balk at the task of learning about symbolism, they can come to realize and appreciate the power and importance of symbols. Dana began her introduction of symbolism with an object—a music box. She showed it to her students and then said:

> "This music box looks like a piano and it plays music. It *is* a music box. But it *is actually much more.* This object symbolizes my relationship with my grandmother. When I was a little girl, I used to rush into her house, wind the key, and watch it with her. We would sit and listen to the music. I can still picture it now. Everything about this music box reminds me of those moments sitting with her—the way it feels in my hands, the tension and tightness in my hand when I wind the key, and especially the music as it moves quickly at first and then slowly, as it unwinds. This music box is a symbol. It is a music box, but it is *more than that* to me. It is a symbol because it is *more than what it seems to be.* There is a greater meaning, or purpose, represented in this object."

At this point, it is often helpful for students to brainstorm objects that are symbolic to them. Many students will cite their favorite stuffed animal or an object they've had since birth. Encourage students to think about what something *is* and what it *represents.* It is *more* than just the object. This is symbolism.

Mystery Bag

Most students are familiar with the symbolic nature of certain animals (a lion, mouse, dog, etc.). Their understanding comes from their experiences with pets, picture books, and multimedia (TV, advertisements, movies, etc.). After assessing your students' understanding of common literary symbols, you may find it helpful to begin with hands-on, concrete activities that help students brainstorm and begin to generate ideas. We have used the activity "Mystery Bag" to spark students' interest in symbols and to uncover additional information about their prior knowledge. For this activity, bring in a bag filled with objects from the classroom and your home, as well as pictures cut from magazines. For example, you might include: an apple, a picture of a dog, a picture of lightning, a seed, and a picture of a garden. As you hold up each item, ask your students what each item might *represent,* or *symbolize*. This helps you to understand what they know about symbolism and what you need to teach next. In addition, we have used picture books, such as *Horton Hatches the Egg, The Lorax*, or *The Sneetches* by Dr. Seuss, to further assess.

Charting Symbols

We usually begin teaching symbolism by creating a chart with common categories: animals, important objects, and weather. Next, we model for our students how to notice which words might go into these categories as we read a text. For example, if we were reading *Horton Hatches the Egg* by Dr. Seuss, we would put *elephant* into the animal column, and *egg* into the important objects column. Creating interactive charts, like the ones in Figure 4.4, is a great way to engage your students. Here we've created two charts, one that reflects students' ideas about symbols in shared texts or in the current read-aloud, and another that allows students to share the symbols they find during their independent reading (see Figure 4.4).

Once students have experience locating symbols in texts, we can ask them to generate ideas about what those words might symbolize (out of context). After that, we might have our students name other texts (stories, images, or songs) that use these symbols. For example, let's say the symbol was a frog. First, we would encourage students to think about the frog as simply a frog. What is special about a frog? It transforms, physically, from a tadpole (living underwater) to a frog (that can live on land). This metamorphosis makes a frog a special type of animal. Next, we think about frogs in popular fairy tales and stories. Students recognize that these stories are about transformations. Simply by considering the frog, outside of a text, students can see that it is a remarkable animal. But by adding a frog to a text, we can see that symbolism is about transformation. Following the thinking in this way allows us to know which students have prior knowledge about the symbolic nature of these words and their ability to reference texts that feature these symbols. We know that if the majority of our students can cite texts that contain these symbols, *and* they can identify the meaning of a symbol, then we must provide instruction that expands their repertoire of symbols.

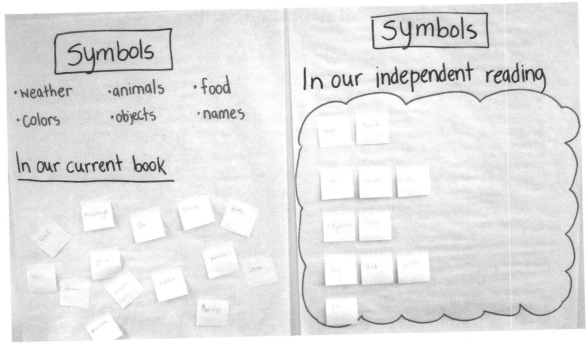

Figure 4.4 Interactive Symbolism Chart

Using Digital Texts

A great way to launch symbolism is to use video clips from animated movies, such as DisneyPixar's short film collections or clips from movies found on YouTube. You can find recommendations for particularly symbolic clips in the digital bins. One terrific

digitalbins.wordpress
.com/symbolism

short film is DisneyPixar's *La Luna*, which is about a boy, his father, and his grandfather working together. The film is filled with symbolism and provides many opportunities for students to locate symbols. We've also used movie clips from children's movies such as *E.T.*, *Shrek*, and *The Wizard of Oz*.

Teaching Interpretation: Symbolism

When *is* a seed just a seed? When is it something more? In this section, the work that students do to decipher whether or not something is a symbol involves having them do detective work to uncover patterns. The hardest part of interpreting symbols can be finding text evidence. This is due to the very definition of a symbol—an idea that is not stated outright. While some students may relish the task of identifying what is not said, others may find it frustrating. Students will need to rely on their keen inferential skills to determine the meaning of symbols, and then use the Interpretation Framework to experiment, weigh, and assess their evidence. Because of its nebulous nature, finding text evidence to support theories about symbolism will require students to pay close attention to the text. They will need to notice recurring images and ideas, detect patterns, make connections between different parts of a text, gather multiple pieces of evidence, and debate their claims with their peers. This work is demonstrated in the following sample lesson.

Identifying Text Evidence

To begin identifying text evidence, help students understand that they are on the lookout for specific types of symbols. As we did in the "Launching" section, you may want to create a chart with categories of symbols. For novice readers, these may include animals, important objects, and weather. For advanced readers, these may include nature, light/dark, names, colors, and settings. As teachers, it is important to acknowledge that the work of analyzing symbols is complex and that it is our job to make it concrete with strategies. Return to Figure 4.2 for a chart of symbols you might want your students to look for and analyze.

Model for students how to notice types of symbols by reading closely, and remind them to jot on a sticky note when they think they've found a symbol. They should include the page numbers where they found symbols because those pages may contain text evidence that will help them create interpretations. Encourage students to ask themselves, "Why might the author have chosen this particular symbol?"

Finding Text Evidence That *Shows* Symbolism

After students locate symbols in the text, they need to find relevant evidence to support their claim. Students begin this work by brainstorming ideas about the symbol (see Figure 4.5). Remind students to think about the meaning of the symbol outside of the text first. Think back to *The Lotus Seed* pre-assessment Dana did with her class, for example. Although her students recognized the seed as important, they did not first consider *why* a seed was selected or what is symbolic about a seed. Instead, her students went straight to the text and did not stop to think about what is symbolic about a seed, outside of the text. If the students had stopped to consider

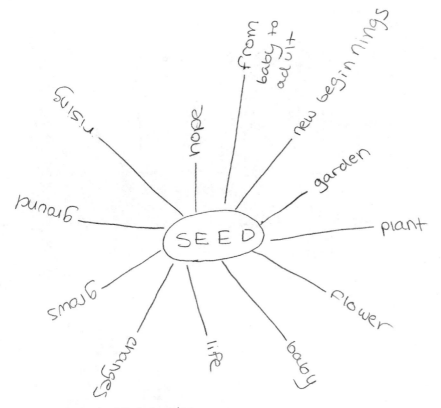

Figure 4.5 Student Brainstorming

what is important about a seed, they would have realized that it changes and grows. A seed can also be transported from one location to another, and it can be planted and transplanted. It is small and strong, bundled tight and waiting. A seed carries metaphors even without a text. Students must brainstorm their ideas *before* they can find text evidence.

You may want to use the Constructing an Interpretation interactive chart to help your students develop initial claims about symbols (see Figure 4.6). Here is an example of brainstorming for ideas of what a seed might symbolize. First, students generated ideas, then they brainstormed evidence to support their ideas in the "Experimenting" section of the chart. Last, students sorted their evidence in the "Rethinking" section to see which ideas have the most evidence. Those that came under "Little Evidence" were rethought and even discarded. Once students brainstorm ideas and create an initial claim about what the symbol means outside of a text, they are ready to be on the lookout for what the symbol means within a text.

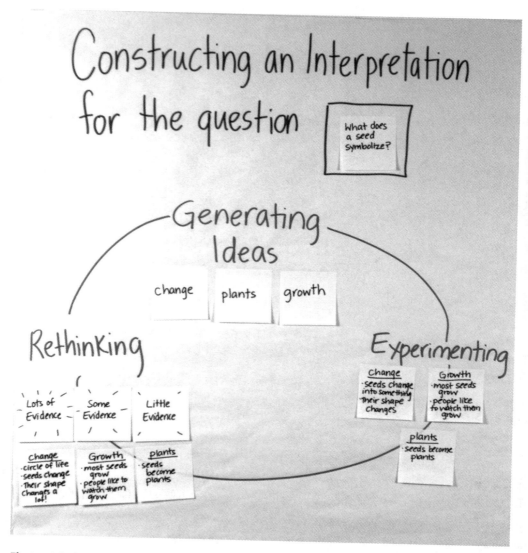

Figure 4.6 Interpretation Framework Chart

How do students find text evidence that *shows* symbolism? First, they establish an initial claim about what they believe their symbol might represent. Next, they need to ask themselves text-evidence questions such as, "Where is the symbol in the text?" "How do the characters feel about it?" "What role does the symbol play in the plot?" and "Does the symbol cause anything to happen in the story?" Once students ask themselves these questions, they can flag examples in their book with sticky notes or annotations. In addition, you may want them to complete a symbolism

graphic organizer to keep track of symbols throughout the text. Encourage students to be looking for different types of symbols, such as animals, weather, color, nature, special objects, and
language that is repeated. For example, while reading the novel *Where the Mountain Meets the
Moon* by Grace Lin, students might identify symbols such as dragons, peaches, the moon, and
the color green. Encourage students to note each symbol with a page number and generate a few
ideas about its symbolism (see Figure 4.7).

Possible Symbol	Page #s	Generating Ideas: What might it symbolize?
Buffalo Boy	Page 118	- hunger - domesticity - love - kind
Colors, Green, purple, Blue, Black, Pink	Page 118	- Soil - mountain - brick - love - heart
Coins	Page 120	- blue bowl - heart of Minli - fish - tried Buffalo Boy - love-giving things - generosity with hope and - peach thinking nothing in return - quick thinking
Peach / monkey \ vender	page 120	- greed - wealth - power - fortunate - love
peach Pit	page 71	- seed - growth - transformation - love

Figure 4.7 Student Graphic Organizer

Summarizing, Paraphrasing, and Quoting Text Evidence

As students locate direct quotations in the text that support their claims, remind them that text evidence can take different forms. This means that students can cite text evidence by summarizing a portion of the text or an entire novel, or they can paraphrase what a character has said or done. This is particularly important when students are writing about symbolism because oftentimes the plot or a chapter needs to be summarized in order to show *why* or *how* something is representative of a larger idea in the text.

You may want to create a chart that delineates the different ways students can write about text evidence. These include direct quotations, paraphrasing a quote or small segment of a text, or summarizing a large portion of a text. It is important for students to become proficient in using these three types of text evidence to support their claims, so they can talk about both large and small portions of text.

After locating text evidence, students are ready to create interpretations. In the following sample lesson, we will show you strategies to help guide your readers through the Interpretation Framework process.

Sample Lesson

This lesson describes the type of work you might do with your students when teaching them how to find text-based evidence to support their claims. We have chosen *Where the Mountain Meets the Moon* by Grace Lin for this work. This sample lesson is designed to help students construct interpretations about symbols. Students will focus on *what* the symbol represents and ask themselves, "How does this symbol play a larger role in the text? How is the author using this symbol?"

LESSON

SNAPSHOT

Lesson Snapshot: Symbolism

CCSS: RL.3.4, 4.4, 5.4, 6.4, 7.4, 8.4

Teaching Objectives:

- Students will construct interpretations about symbols in the text.
- Students will support their claims with relevant text evidence.

Materials:
- Select a text rich with symbolism or choose from the Text Recs list
- Symbolism Categories Chart

Steps:

1. Have students bring their initial claims about the symbols they are identifying in the text to the meeting area.

2. With the whole class, discuss the purpose of the lesson "How to construct interpretations about *why* the author has created a symbol" and introduce the Symbolism Categories Chart.

3. Model how to use the chart and construct an interpretation using a familiar text.

4. Model analyzing the symbol you have found in relation to the whole text and the author's intent (the *why* and the *how*). Demonstrate connecting your ideas about the symbol and writing an initial interpretation.

5. Encourage your students to try this work on their own or in small groups.

(To differentiate instruction, refer to the Novice and Advanced Readers suggestions located toward the end of this chapter.)

The Deeper Meaning of Symbols

Once students have generated initial claims about symbols in the text (using a graphic organizer), encourage them to expand on their thinking about symbols to include considering the author's intent and the larger ideas embedded in the text. "*Why* did the author choose this symbol?" "How is it revealing a deeper message or idea?" This can be challenging work at first. In order to make this work concrete and accessible for students, start with what students already know. Review the types of symbols your students have been searching for (animals, weather, colors, food, etc.), then say to your students:

"We have been learning how to identify symbols in the text and generating initial claims about what they represent. Today we are going to learn how to create interpretations about why the author has created the symbol. What is its purpose in the text?"

Next, introduce a chart with new categories to your students. These categories can include: "Emotions/Feelings," "Relationships," "Transformation and Change," and "Conditions."

Emotions/Feelings (Grief, Love, Desperation)	Relationships (Family, Friends)	Transformation and Change (Growth, Change, Destruction)	Conditions (Poverty, Illness, Popularity)

Figure 4.8 Symbolism Categories

Explain that these categories reveal the author's intent. They are the reasons *why* an author might create a symbol. Give your students examples they are familiar with—such as a frog—to reveal a change or transformation in the text. You might say, "How does the author use a frog as a symbol? The author uses a frog as a symbol of transformation." Likewise, a quilt, necklace, or picture might go in the "Relationships" category because they symbolize relationships between family members or friends. Although there are more categories, we recommend starting with these four because we have found them to be the most accessible to students. This work is abstract, it pushes students' thinker deeper and encourages students to think about how they will interpret the symbols and the author's intent.

After modeling how to use the chart with the four categories, encourage your students to consider the symbols they've been noticing. Have your students talk to each other about the categories for their symbols. Some students may find that their symbol could fall under more than one category. To support your students' growth with this work, encourage them to ask, "Why this particular symbol?" Students will generate many different claims about symbols, and some of their ideas may be wild and unfounded, so it is important for them to get peer and teacher feedback. This is challenging work because it requires not only identifying what a symbol means, but how that symbol reveals the author's intent through characters and plot development, as well as how it illuminates universal ideas and themes.

Supporting Our Students

Throughout this process you may discover that some students require additional support to make this leap. For example, one student, Cassie, chose to investigate the moon as a symbol. She began by brainstorming what she knew about the moon (see Figure 4.9). Cassie's initial claim was that the moon symbolized wisdom. As Cassie gathered text evidence she became even more confident that the moon symbolized wisdom. In this lesson, however, she felt sure that the moon

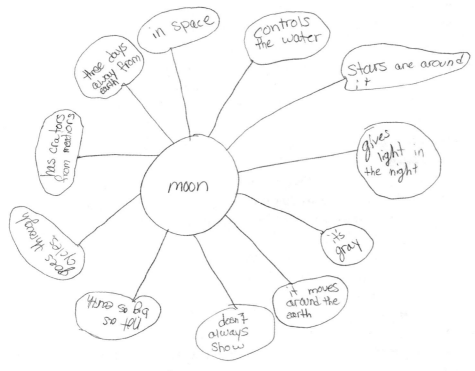

Figure 4.9 Cassie's Brainstorming

fell into the "Transformation and Change" category, but she was not sure how to connect her two ideas: wisdom and transformation.

This is reflective of the type of work students have to do in order to make the leap to get to the author's intent and main message. For Cassie to connect her two ideas and move her claim forward, she needed to think about *why* the moon was a transformational symbol. Students like Cassie may need prompts to guide their thinking.

During this lesson, Cassie thought about the moon and its cycles and how it changes a little each night. This led her to think more about how *change* and *transformation* might be important in the text. Which characters changed? Next, Cassie thought about how her ideas about wisdom related to

Why did the author choose this symbol?

How does the symbolism reveal BIG ideas in the text?

How does the symbolism connect to the conflicts in the text?

transformation. She pushed herself to think about how wisdom *changes* or *transforms* characters in the text. This finally led Cassie to think about how the main character changes throughout the text.

After experimenting with her claim, Cassie was ready to discuss how the symbol of the moon reveals the author's main messages in the text. Cassie talked with her classmates about how her interpretation fit within the larger context of the author's purpose and the central ideas of the text.

"I think Grace Lin uses the moon to show how Minli changes," Cassie said.

"How?" asked Molly.

"Well, see here at the beginning of the story, she is unhappy with her life, and she is trying to find the Man of the Moon in order to change her family's fate—see that's change. And by the end of the book, well you know what happens, she learns that she should be happy with what she already has."

"So how does the moon show she changes?" Molly asked.

"It doesn't *show* that she changes. But it symbolizes wisdom, and Minli changes because of the wisdom she gets, you know?" Cassie responded.

"I think I get it," Molly said.

"What about the author?" Sophie asked.

"I think Grace Lin wants us all to learn a lesson, you know? Like a moral. Be happy with what you already have," Cassie ended.

You may find that students' conversations need to be guided deeper. Ask students to make connections to other texts that might contain similar symbols.

Generating Thesis Statements

In the next lesson, have students refine their interpretations and write thesis statements. Keeping this process as concrete and straightforward as possible, students can use their claims as a starting off point. Cassie's claim was:

"The moon symbolizes wisdom and transformation."

This thesis statement is clear and concise. It is a terrific jumping off point for a literary paragraph or an essay. However, Cassie can make this thesis statement even stronger by incorporating her ideas about Minli's character development and the author's intent. A revision of Cassie's thesis statement might be:

"Grace Lin uses the moon as a symbol of transformation and wisdom in order
to reveal how Minli's character changes."

Like Cassie's claim about the moon, students can choose many different symbols in the
text. If your students are writing paragraphs or essays about their ideas, it is important to have
them use the mnemonic "BAM!" in their topic sentences (Book title, Author's Name, Main
idea of the paragraph) and to discuss why the symbol is important in a text. Here is Cassie's
first draft of her paragraph (see Figure 4.10).

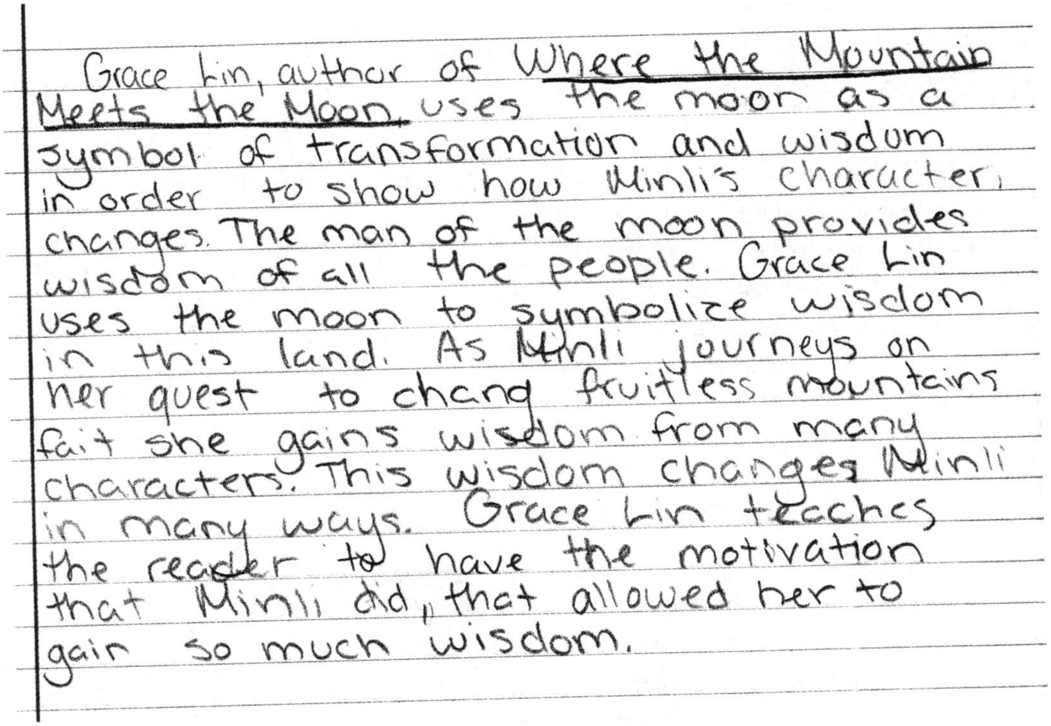

Grace Lin, author of Where the Mountain
Meets the Moon, uses the moon as a
symbol of transformation and wisdom
in order to show how Minli's character,
changes. The man of the moon provides
wisdom of all the people. Grace Lin
uses the moon to symbolize wisdom
in this land. As Minli journeys on
her quest to chang fruitless mountains
fait she gains wisdom from many
characters. This wisdom changes Minli
in many ways. Grace Lin teaches
the reader to have the motivation
that Minli did, that allowed her to
gain so much wisdom.

Figure 4.10 Cassie's First Draft

The Interpretation Framework Process

GENERATING IDEAS: Students will consider whether objects identified in a text might represent, or symbolize, bigger ideas. Students can consider whether an object appears only once or reoccurs throughout the text when determining if it could be a symbol. Remind students that symbolism means an idea—an emotion, a relationship, change or transformation, or a condition. Students may move directly from generating ideas to either rethinking or experimenting in the Interpretation Framework.

RETHINKING: As students begin generating ideas about symbolism, encourage them to look for more than one interpretation. An important goal for students is to develop the habit of exploring more than one possibility, rather than locking into a singular point of view. This can be challenging for some students who feel certain—and strongly—about their initial claims. The act of thinking flexibly is essential to students' growth as learners and to strengthening their claims and interpretations.

EXPERIMENTING: Finding text evidence to support their ideas about symbolism is an opportunity for students to test the waters and determine whether or not their claim has validity. This may push them back to the process of rethinking if they discover that they cannot support their ideas. If students believe that they have found that evidence, ask them to rank this text support, as Lucy Calkins in *Tackling Complex Texts* (2010) recommends, using a "strong, stronger, strongest continuum" to help them discover which evidence is truly supportive and which evidence is superficial.

Looking Across Texts

Once your students are able to identify symbols and what they symbolize in a text, they can begin to look across texts to analyze how other authors use common symbols. For example, students noticed that a goldfish was a recurring symbol in many of the texts they read, including *Out of My Mind* by Sharon Draper, *Rules* by Cynthia Lord, and *Where the Mountain Meets the Moon* by Grace Lin. Students generated initial claims about the goldfish and then began discussing the authors' intent.

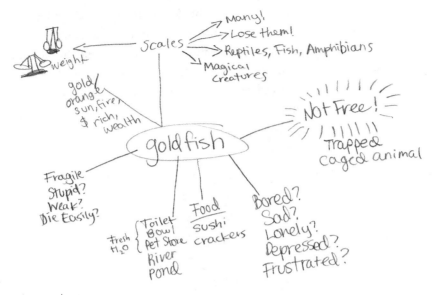

Figure 4.11 Brainstorming

Strategies for Novice Readers

Using sticky notes to annotate a text is a great strategy for novice readers. Sticky notes are removable, can be transferred from one chapter to another, and can be removed from the text and stored as examples of how to cite and note text evidence. Encourage your novice readers to use sticky notes to flag their ideas (claims, evidence, rethinking) in their text. Then have your readers choose their strongest evidence from among their sticky notes. These sticky notes should then be stored in their reader's notebooks as examples of how to make interpretations. This is especially valuable when working with symbolism, because students can look back at their sticky notes to remember the kinds of symbols they found in previous texts (animals, nature, colors, names, etc.).

A reader's notebook is another essential tool to help novice readers construct interpretations about symbolism.

Encourage students to use their reader's notebook to note their ideas about symbols after they read, looking back over their sticky notes or annotations. A good time for students to jot down their ideas is at the end of a reading workshop. Set aside five minutes for students to look back over their ideas and write a quick entry of their thoughts. This might take the form of a list or a short paragraph. Here are two student examples from reader's notebooks after reading *Esperanza Rising* by Pam Muñoz Ryan (see Figures 4.12 and 4.13).

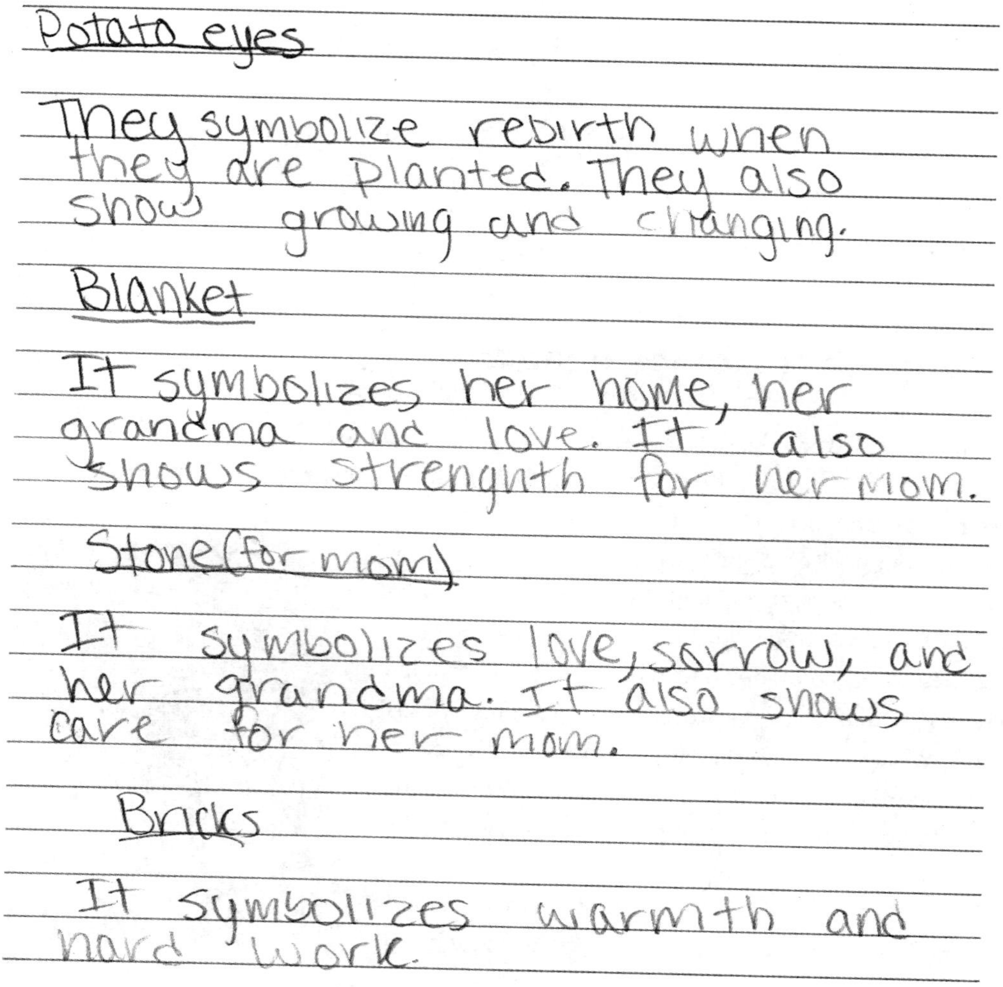

Potato eyes

They symbolize rebirth when they are planted. They also show growing and changing.

Blanket

It symbolizes her home, her grandma and love. It also shows strength for her mom.

Stone (for mom)

It symbolizes love, sorrow, and her grandma. It also shows care for her mom.

Bricks

It symbolizes warmth and hard work.

Figure 4.12 Student Work Interpreting Symbols

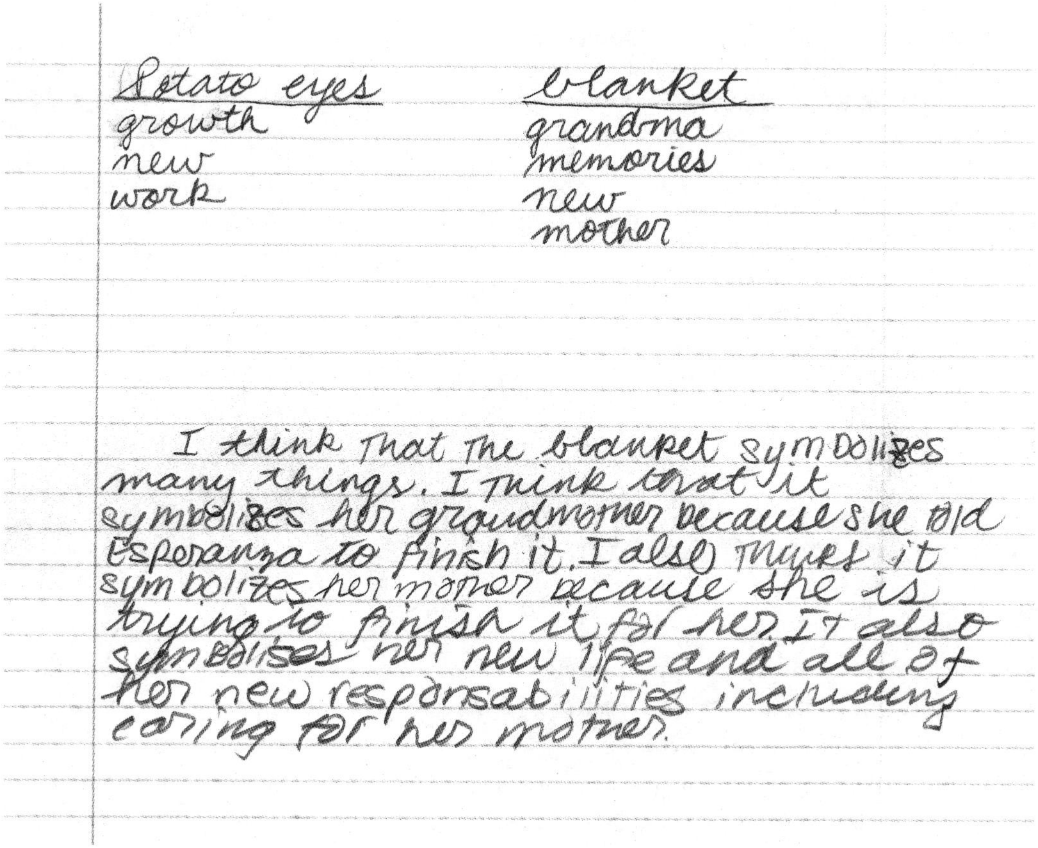

Potato eyes
growth
new
work

blanket
grandma
memories
new
mother

I think that the blanket symbolizes many things. I think that it symbolizes her grandmother because she told Esperanza to finish it. I also think it symbolizes her mother because she is trying to finish it for her. It also symbolizes her new life and all of her new responsabilities including caring for her mother.

Figure 4.13 Student Interpreting Symbols

If . . . Try . . .

HELPING NOVICE READERS CREATE INTERPRETATIONS ABOUT SYMBOLISM

If . . .	Try . . .
Students have found a symbol but cannot identify its symbolism . . .	Demonstrate how you find a symbol and then consider what it might represent—an emotion? A thing? A relationship? Refer to a chart or graphic organizer with examples of symbolism. Model for your students and then have them try this work with relatively simple symbols first (e.g., a tree, quilt, dog, lion, mouse, flower, etc.).

Figure 4.14 If . . . Try . . .

(continues)

Students are struggling to dig deeper to identify the author's purpose . . .	Prompt them with questions such as "Why did the author choose this particular symbol?" "What BIG idea or theme is the author trying to reveal?" or "What does the author want us to learn?" Encourage students to "try on" different lenses. Refer to the Critical Lenses chart (see Figure 3.2).
Students are having difficulty honing their interpretations or making thesis statements . . .	Begin by having your students state what the symbol is and what it represents. Encourage your students to state their interpretation in this manner. For their thesis statement, you may want them to include *why*, *how*, or the author's purpose.

Figure 4.14 If . . . Try . . . *(continued)*

Strategies for Advanced Readers

Once your advanced readers have identified symbols in the text, considered the author's purpose, and examined their claim from different angles, they are ready to connect their idea about symbolism to other literary elements, such as perspective and theme. Use the prompts and questions below to guide your advanced readers.

As your students begin forming ideas about symbolism, encourage your advanced readers to jot down their ideas in their reader's notebooks as free responses or as paragraphs. Use the symbolism chart found at the beginning of this chapter (see Figure 4.2) to differentiate the symbols your readers should be searching for. For example, some of our students look for common literary symbols such as animals, objects, and colors, while our more advanced readers look for juxtapositions of settings, passage of time, and power. A great place to begin is by encouraging your students to take note of characters' names. We find it helpful to have a baby names book handy in our classroom or a link to a baby names website. Remind students that authors choose names that have symbolic meanings. Often, these names help take our readers' thinking deeper and guide them to start thinking about symbols such as biblical allusions,

Guiding Prompts and Questions For Advanced Readers

1. Think about the author's purpose.

2. How does the symbolism relate to the external and internal conflicts?

3. How does the symbolism reveal themes in the text?

good versus evil, and characters' actions. Take, for example, the characters in *Esperanza Rising*. Here's an example of a student analyzing the symbolism of the characters' names (see Figure 4.15). Just by looking up the meaning of the characters' names, this student was able to uncover the deep symbolism of the characters and the author's intent when creating those characters.

In the book, Esperanza Rising, by Pam Muñoz the names chosen have a significant importance. To begin, Esperanza's name means "hope." Esperanza's hope, of being able to live in the conditions and hardships she is experiencing, is nessecary in order to continue her life. Miguel, another character, has a name that means "like God". I believe God is supposed to help people through their difficulties in life. Miguel helps guide Esperanza through her new life. Miguel does many great things for Esperanza to make her feel comfortable and happy. Also, Marta and Isabel are important characters in the book. Marta means "sorrow-ful" and "friend to Jesus". Also, Isabel means "consecrated to God". These characters both relate to God, showing they each help Esperanza in different ways. Isabel guided Esperanza to realize that objects are not important, but it is the meaning of the object that is special. Marta led Esperanza to learn that family is most important. Esperanza's mother, Ramona, name means "wise protector". She supports Esperanza through her life, as well as her own. She tries to protect Esperanza from realizing the transition is difficult for her mother also. In conclusion, the characters' names all symbolize their importance in the book towards helping Esperanza rise through her new life.

Figure 4.15 Literary Analysis

This sixth-grade student made connections between the characters' names and their roles as she analyzed symbolism.

Although you can use novels and picture books to spur your advanced readers' thinking, you can also use digital texts, such as animated short films, photographs, advertisements, and songs. Using digital texts is one way to introduce your students to symbolism. It's also a great way to keep your students engaged and take their thinking to a new level. We have used the DisneyPixar animated short film *La Luna* to strengthen our students' understanding of symbolism. Once they have identified symbols in the film (e.g., the boat, moon, ladder, hats, etc.), they can begin to analyze the symbolism inherent in the story. One student wrote about the symbolism of the moon in relation to the generations of people in the boat. This seventh-grade student jotted notes in his reader's notebook and then wrote an analytical paragraph (see Figure 4.16).

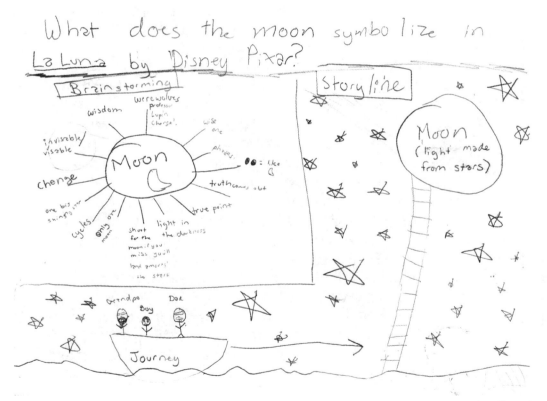

Figure 4.16A Student Brainstorming

(continues)

"Shoot for the moon, if you miss you'll land amoung the stars,"—Les Brown. In La Luna you can land amoung both. In the movie La Luna by Disney Pixar the moon is very symbolic as it is in many other stories. Authors put symbols, such as moon in books, movies, or stories to create a deeper meaning One of the things the moon symbolizes is change. For example, in Harry Potter and the Prisoner of Azkaban Professor Lupin, the werewolf, changes every time he sees the moon. In La Luna you can tell it symbolizes change because all of men in the boat are from the same family have changed from generation to generation. Another thing the moon symbolizes is the lightness in the dark or hope. The moon is literally is the light in the darkness; you can only see it clearly in the darkest times. A lot of times you hear the expression, "No matter how lonely you feel we'll always know we'll be looking at the same moon." That quote shows how in some cases it is the light in the dark which brings two people together. The most important thing the moon symbolizes is the true point. That might sound weird at first, but it is true. There is only one moon within all of the stars, just like there is only one point in all stories and lots of other things. Moons are important symbols in lots of books and storylines espeially La Luna. With out them a lot of stories wouldn't have a true meaning and/or plot.

Figure 4.16B Analysis of Symbols Across Texts *(continued)*

If . . . Try . . .

HELPING ADVANCED READERS CREATE INTERPRETATIONS ABOUT SYMBOLISM

If . . .	Try . . .
Students have found a symbol but cannot identify its symbolism . . .	Refer to the chart or graphic organizer with categories of symbols (Feelings, Relationships, Transformation, Conditions, etc.—Figure 4.8). Use this chart to model for your students how to push past the identification of a symbol and initial thoughts about what it represents to locate categories of symbols and finding the bigger ideas.
Students are making claims that are strong but could be even stronger . . .	Encourage students to identify the many characteristics of a symbol and to apply this to their ideas. For example, a seed changes and grows, but it is also small, can be transported, and may only grow under specific conditions. Ask students to consider how several characteristics can strengthen their claim.
Students are forming a strong claim, finding strong evidence, but not rethinking . . .	You might begin by modeling the process of rethinking. You could say, "Even though you have a strong claim and strong evidence, it is important to always look for different angles. Try a different viewpoint and see how that affects your claim."

Figure 4.17 If . . . Try . . .

Planning a Year of Teaching Symbolism

You can weave lessons about symbolism into any reading unit during your school year. Some years, we have taught a lesson about symbolism in the very first read-aloud on the first day of school. Other years, we've held off until the end of the second or third reading unit. You can customize how you want to teach symbolism in your reading curriculum. For example, you might teach symbolism intensely during one reading unit, or you might teach one or two lessons about symbolism in each of your reading units. If you choose to teach symbolism across the school year, your lessons might look like the following:

Symbolism Lessons Across the School Year

September: Introduce the idea of symbolism in read-alouds or during your first reading unit. Teach your students to keep their eyes open for repetition and common literary symbols.

October: In your new reading unit, encourage students to identify symbols in their texts and to *generate* initial claims and *experiment* with text evidence.

November: This month, students focus on finding the best text evidence that supports their claims about symbolism, and have them rank order their evidence from weakest to strongest.

December: Drive students' thinking deeper by having them *rethink* their claims and debate them with their peers. Continue having students look for symbols in each text they read.

January: Challenge students to categorize their interpretations about symbols based on the four main categories: Feelings/Emotions, Relationships, Transformation/Change, and Conditions.

February: Students should be able to identify symbols in texts and make initial claims. Encourage students to write thesis statements about their claims that bridge their ideas about the symbol with the category their symbol falls under.

March: Focus on students' ability to journey through the Interpretation Framework on their own. Can they generate ideas about symbolism, experiment with evidence, and rethink their claims?

April: Breathe new life into your study of symbolism by introducing a variety of new texts, including poems, song lyrics, and films. Have students read across texts for common symbols.

May: As your students locate symbols in their texts, differentiate your instruction to push both your novice and advanced readers' thinking deeper by using the suggestions in the If . . . Try . . . boxes.

June: End your year of teaching symbolism with a review of the Interpretation Framework process.

Possible Symbol	Page Number(s)	Generating Ideas: What might it symbolize?

Figure 4.18

Supporting Ideas About Symbols

SYMBOL: _____

Generating Ideas: It could symbolize . . .

Experimenting with Evidence (Pick three ideas and test for strong evidence.)

#1 Evidence on pages _____

#2 Evidence on pages _____

#3 Evidence on pages _____

Strongest Theory =

Figure 4.19

5

Theme

*Connecting to
Universal Ideas
Embedded in Texts*

Do you ever find *yourself dreading teaching a certain
topic? Feeling insecure about your teaching because you
know that you're not quite sure how to make it concrete
and accessible for your students? We used to feel this way
about teaching our students how to find themes.*

*We confess. We used to research the term theme prior
to teaching it to our students. Dana would read Wikipedia,
hoping to learn how to define theme. A "central topic,"
Wikipedia would say, "a concept the author is trying to
point out. Not to be confused with whatever message,
moral, or commentary it may send." This definition seemed
abstract and vague. Also, Dana wasn't sure she agreed
with it. A central topic that was not the author's main
message? She knew she needed to find more information
about theme. Sonja also researched. She found herself at
Learner.org. This website states: "In fiction, the theme is
not intended to teach or preach. In fact, it is not presented
directly at all. You extract it from the characters, action, and
setting that make up the story. In other words, you must
figure out the theme yourself." This was equally confusing.
How do you teach students to find something that isn't
presented directly? We both googled "teaching theme."
What we found was astonishing. There were multiple*

132

"Help" websites with the heading "How do I teach theme?" posted by teachers all over the country. We visited a lot of these sites and realized that many teachers were asking the same questions we were. As we finished our research, we felt the same way teachers do all over the country—confused about how to teach theme.

As teachers, we know how frustrating it can be to teach an abstract concept while trying to make it concrete and accessible for our students. We want to present ideas in ways that students can understand, explore, and use independently. We want our teaching to transfer across genres, texts, and content areas. Most importantly, we want our teaching to be meaningful. Theme is arguably one of the most significant literary elements in a text. Determining theme requires students to draw inferences and think beyond the small details explicitly given in a text. Students will need to determine the author's message, consider the connections that can be made across different texts, and relate these ideas to their own lives. Today, we feel more confident about teaching theme, but like many of our colleagues, we are still on a journey of delivering instruction that makes theme accessible to all learners. We continue to grapple with the questions: "What is theme?" "How do we teach theme to our students?" "How can we assess their understanding of theme and deepen it?"

Rationale and Common Core State Standards Connection

The Common Core standards require students beginning in third grade to determine and compare and contrast themes (RL3.9, 4.2, 4.9, 5.2, 5.9, 6.2, 6.5, 7.2, 8.2, 8.9). In *Pathways to the Common Core*, Calkins, Ehrenworth, and Lehman note "The Common Core leads us away from the mindset that texts are about one 'main idea'" (2012, p. 80). As students are required to tackle more complex texts, Calkins recommends that teachers encourage students to investigate multiple main ideas in order to analyze theme. It's important to note that the Common Core standards do not define theme. However, the standards do require students to identify themes across texts, compare and contrast themes, and analyze themes. This can be problematic for educators who view theme as a vague concept. Furthermore, there can be varying definitions of theme.

If there is no clear definition of *theme* and no consensus on its meaning, how then do we teach our students to do this work required by the Common Core? To add further confusion, there are several buzzwords that are used synonymously with theme. These may include: *topic, idea, main idea, big idea, main message, author's message, moral of the story, purpose of the story, patterns, claim,* or *thesis.* Students may be asked, "What is this story about?" Lucy Calkins (2010) describes theme as the "grit of the story" (p. 165), and Stephanie Harvey describes it as something you "feel in your gut" (p. 109). For many novice teachers, theme can feel like an elusive concept, leading them to wonder, "What exactly is *theme* and how do I teach it?" We turned to experts like Calkins and Harvey and their extensive body of research and writing in order to make the process of understanding and teaching theme possible.

Getting Ready

Pre-Assessment

digitalbins.wordpress
.com/theme

To assess your students' understanding of theme, you can use the texts in the Text Recs list or a text found in the digital bins. We find that using a picture book or a short text can be a quick and simple way to assess our students' understanding of theme. Occasionally, we include a question about theme on other pre-assessments (for symbolism, perspective, etc.) in order to have a snapshot of our students' existing knowledge of theme. You can use the prompts below with any text to ask your students questions about theme.

1. What is a theme in this text? Use text evidence to support your claim.

2. Why did the author create this theme?

3. Are there other themes in this text? If so, what are they?

Once you have assessed your students' current understanding, you may find that they have varying notions of theme. This will require you to differentiate your instruction in order to meet the needs of all your learners. Toward the end of this chapter, you will find If . . . Try . . . boxes that contain suggestions for Novice and Advanced readers to help you alter your instruction according to the needs of your students.

Creating text sets can also give students opportunities to do the higher-level analysis and comparative work called for by the Common Core. These sets allow students to compare and contrast themes across texts. You can create text sets around similar topics, issues, and themes. For example, you might create text sets around civil rights, adaptations, or growing up. In order to create these sets you can use a variety of texts including: video clips, photographs, *Time for Kids* articles, short texts, poems, and picture books. We know that the task of pulling texts together can be time-consuming and at times challenging, therefore we suggest dividing up this task among colleagues. For example, if each teacher on a team creates a text set, you will have a total of two or more text sets. There are other resources you can turn to as well, such as the text sets posted on the Reading and Writing Project's website(www.readingandwritingproject.com). In addition, resources such as Harvey Daniels' *Texts and Lessons for Teaching Literature* (2013), as well as Daniels' *Texts and Lessons for Content-Area Reading* (2011) are filled with resources you can use to create your own text sets.

Text Recs: Dana and Sonja's Book Bins

We love using the following texts in our classrooms when teaching theme:

Picture Books	Chapter Books	Nonfiction, Short Stories, Poetry
Each Kindness by Jacqueline Woodson	*Seedfolks* by Paul Fleischman	"The Bats" by Alma Flor Ada
Wilma Unlimited by Kathleen Krull	*F is For Freedom* by Roni Schotter	"Eleven" by Sandra Cisneros
Weslandia by Paul Fleischman	*The Crazy Man* by Pamela Porter	"A Dream Deferred" by Langston Hughes
Thank you, Mr. Falker by Patricia Polacco	*Hatchet* by Gary Paulsen	"On Turning Ten" by Billy Collins
Passage to Freedom: The Sugihara Story by Ken Mochizuki	*The Trumpet of the Swan* by E. B. White	"Edna Mae: First Lesson in Prejudice" by Sandra Warren
Faithful Elephants by Yukio Tsuchiya	*Wonder* by R. J. Palacio	
	Maniac Magee by Jerry Spinelli	"My Grandmother's Hair" by Cynthia Rylant
The Widow's Broom by Chris Van Allsburg	*The Cay* by Theodore Taylor	"His First Flight" by Liam O'Flaherty
Silent Music: A Story of Baghdad by James Rumford	*My Side of the Mountain* by Jean Craighead George	"Hands of the Maya" by Rachel Crandell
	How Tia Lola Came to Stay by Julia Alvarez	"Every Living Thing" by Cynthia Rylant
One Thousand Tracings: Healing the Wounds of World War II by Lita Judge		"Harvesting Hope: The Story of César Chávez" by Kathleen Krull
		"When Marian Sang" by Pam Muñoz Ryan
		"Life Doesn't Frighten Me" by Maya Angelou

Figure 5.1 Text Recs

Launching

"What Is Theme?"

Imagine that you are throwing a birthday party for your eight-year-old nephew. You know he loves the movie *Star Wars*. He's spent hours watching the DVDs, he's collected all of the action figures, and he dresses up for Halloween as Darth Vader. You know it would be perfect to use *Star Wars* as

a theme for his eighth birthday party. To carry out this theme, you go to your local party store and purchase all things *Star Wars*. You buy plates, cups, napkins, balloons, tablecloths, and party favors, all displaying *Stars Wars* characters and logos. In addition, you plan party games featuring lightsabers, scene reenactments with costumes, and a Death Star piñata. The grand finale is a cake that resembles Luke Skywalker. All in all, you have planned the perfect party for this theme. If we were to analyze how your actions support the concept of theme, we might notice the following: 1) Attention to details: characters, objects, and color scheme or setting, 2) Noting patterns: repeated images, phrases, and emotions, 3) Naming the threads that tie it all together: good versus evil, hero versus villain, bravery, problem solving, and fighting for what's right. After analyzing these actions, a definition of theme may begin to emerge.

Looking for patterns across a text is an essential first step to finding a theme. Chris Lehman and Kate Roberts (2013) help students find text evidence by showing them how to gather lists of words, note the structure of a text, pay attention to similarities and differences, and contemplate how this evidence interacts together. Further, Stephanie Harvey and Anne Goudvis (2000) help us construct a strong understanding of theme by sharing the advice they give to students: "We explain to our students that themes are the underlying ideas, morals, and lessons that give the story its texture, depth, and meaning. The themes are rarely written out in the story. We infer themes" (p. 109). Themes can be tied to emotions such as anger, guilt, and joy, which, Harvey and Goudvis explain, helps students *feel* their way to determining the theme. This is a powerful explanation; it makes clear that our students should feel strongly about their ideas in relation to theme. Theme evokes an emotional response. Therefore, we define theme as a thread that runs throughout a text and evokes an emotional response within the reader. How then do we teach our students to notice and latch onto this abstract thread? For some students, this thread may seem invisible because they cannot see it, explicitly, in the text. However, it is there. Our job as educators is to teach students *how* to see it. The following chart illustrates some examples of themes that students may uncover in the texts they read (see Figure 5.2).

Novice	Intermediate	Advanced
friendship	inequality	racial inequality
freedom	injustice	transitions
fairness	growing up/independence	fighting for what's right
love	self-respect	overcoming obstacles
kindness	working together	oppression
cooperation	segregation	repression
family	discrimination	gender bias
bravery	good versus evil	power
sadness	perseverance	privilege
loneliness	responsibility	morality
determination	maturity	breaking/repeating cycles
loyalty	greed	diversity

Figure 5.2 Examples of Themes

You may notice that themes comprise mainly abstract nouns and phrases. This is important, because if students offer ideas that include adjectives (happy, terrifying, annoying), verbs (dance, move, fight), or common nouns (kittens, science, birthday parties), they should be redirected to unearth bigger ideas represented in the text. These ideas should be named using abstract nouns or phrases.

Teaching Interpretation: Theme

Students need to draw upon multiple skills, such as those discussed throughout this book (mood, atmosphere, tone; figurative language; multiple perspectives; and symbolism) and bring them together to construct interpretations about theme. We have created a text set around a familiar topic—birthdays—because sometimes readers are asked to look across texts to think about theme. Creating text sets in the classroom is important because they present students with opportunities to explore a variety of genres, voices, and perspectives, all related to a similar topic. As a result of such intertextual reading, students will be able to bridge ideas across and between texts, search for patterns and disagreements, raise questions inspired by texts and experiences in their own lives, and share and construct knowledge while engaging in discourse around shared texts.

Identifying Text Evidence

Since theme is a thread that runs throughout an entire text, students will be asked to use all their strategies for identifying text evidence. This includes locating text evidence in the form of direct quotations, paraphrasing scenes or paragraphs, or summarizing chapters or even entire texts.

We've experienced two common pitfalls when teaching students to find text evidence for theme. First, students often become swamped in summarizing the plot when finding text evidence to support their claim about theme. To avoid this pitfall and help students differentiate between the events of the story and the big idea of the story, an initial conversation about theme might begin with a discussion of well-known animated movies. For example, you might

Movie Title	Plot	Theme
Beauty and the Beast	The beast is actually a prince who has been cursed until someone falls in love with him.	When it comes to love, what matters is who you are on the inside, not what you look like on the outside.
The Lion King	After the king of the lion pride is killed, his young cub is led to believe that he is responsible for his father's death. He runs away from the pride until one day he realizes that he must return.	The circle of life. There are a variety of experiences in life, both good and bad, that help shape us into the person we are meant to be.
Finding Nemo	A young fish becomes separated from his father, and both of them have to rely on the kindness of new friends to find their way back to each other.	Determination means never giving up until you reach your goal.

Figure 5.3 Sample Theme Chart

discuss the movies *Beauty and the Beast, The Lion King*, and *Finding Nemo*. Create a chart for each movie (see Figure 5.18 for a blank template). Summarize the plot of each movie on the left side, and determine the theme of each movie on the right side. The plot is discussed and then used to determine theme, as opposed to students identifying the plot as the theme.

We've found that while older students who watched these movies several years ago may have forgotten many of the details, what has stayed with them over the years are the themes of these movies. When we ask our students why that might be, they respond by explaining that they identified with several of the characters. Although the characters' particular circumstances differed, our students had an emotional connection to them and they remembered how the movies made them *feel*. These feelings are not bound to a particular detail, plot, or setting, but instead are experienced powerfully by our students and in the world in which they live.

A second pitfall is when students identify one event or moment in the story as a theme and do not look across the entire text for a theme. These students may limit their identification of themes by selecting only one theme in a text. To help students avoid this pitfall, select one of the movies previously discussed, such as *The Lion King* or *Finding Nemo*, and challenge students to consider the possibility of additional themes in the movie. They can begin by recalling specific events from the movie. However, encourage students to consider whether their ideas extend beyond this single event and across the entire movie. Invite students to make a list of their ideas and to discuss and debate them with their peers. Creating an interactive chart, such as our Constructing an Interpretation chart, helps students avoid the pitfall of choosing themes based on one small part of the story (see Figure 5.4).

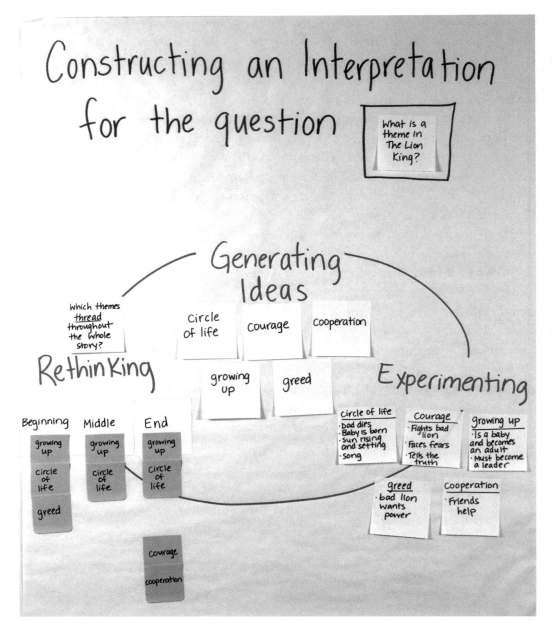

Figure 5.4 Interpretation Framework Chart

Finding Nemo	
Events/Plot	**Themes**
Dory continuing to remember important information, like the address Nemo trying to get out of the tank	Determination
Nemo's father, Marlin, and Dory Marlin and the sea turtles Nemo and the seagulls Nemo and the fish in the tank	Friendship
Nemo and his father, Marlin Sea turtle families	Family
Marlin surviving the shark attack Marlin and Nemo leaving home and going beyond the sea anemone	Bravery

Figure 5.5 Identifying Themes

A chart like this also helps students avoid locking onto the idea that there can be only one theme in a text (see Figure 5.5). A blank version of this chart can be found at the end of this chapter (see Figure 5.19).

While these are certainly not the only challenges students will face when identifying text evidence and themes, these are some common areas of difficulty. The following sample lesson is an example of the work you might do with your students on theme.

Sample Lesson

The three short texts selected for this lesson are the short stories "Eleven" by Sandra Cisneros, "Edna Mae: First Lesson in Prejudice" by Sandra Warren, and the poem "On Turning Ten" by Billy Collins. Using short texts makes this teaching very accessible to students who can be given their own copies of the texts to engage with and annotate in order to do the active, close reading expected of them.

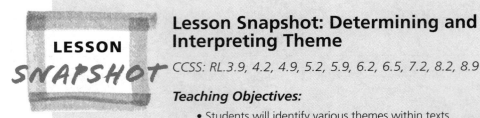

Lesson Snapshot: Determining and Interpreting Theme

CCSS: RL.3.9, 4.2, 4.9, 5.2, 5.9, 6.2, 6.5, 7.2, 8.2, 8.9

Teaching Objectives:

- Students will identify various themes within texts.
- Students will support their claims with relevant text evidence.

Materials:

- A text set of two or three short texts
- Graphic organizers and/or reader's notebooks

Steps:

1. Begin with a pre-reading activity or discussion related to the topic or issue that students will be reading about.
2. Ask students to read texts and annotate them with sticky notes that capture their reactions and responses.
3. Have students organize their thinking about each text on a graphic organizer.
4. Ask students to look across the texts and review their graphic organizers to generate ideas about a theme.
5. Have students select the strongest evidence from each text that supports their ideas about a theme and construct extended responses.

(To differentiate instruction, refer to the Novice and Advanced Readers suggestions located toward the end of this chapter.)

Pre-Reading

If reading across text sets is new to your class, students may benefit from doing this work in small groups prior to doing this work independently. Sonja organized her students into small groups of four or five students. Before they began to read the texts, she asked them to have a pre-reading discussion about birthdays using the following prompt: "When you think about birthdays, which thoughts/images come to mind?" Students took a few minutes to respond to this prompt in their reader's notebooks, and then they discussed their ideas in their small groups.

Sonja listened in on these conversations and jotted down the gist of what came up in each of the groups. She noted the following:

"When I think about birthdays, I think about a day when a person is celebrated for getting one year older and for who they are. I also think about friends, family, joy, and celebrations."

—Ted

"When I think about birthdays, the image in my mind includes cake, balloons, family, presents, food, friends, parties, and sometimes surprises."

—Mara

"When I think about birthdays, I picture chocolate mousse cake and lots of presents. I picture lots of balloons and a party with friends. I picture families going out for dinner and loud music. I picture one happy person excited for their special day."

—Rita

Reading a Text Set

After providing an opportunity for groups to share a few of their ideas with the class, Sonja moved on with the lesson.

"Today you will be reading three short texts about birthdays. Remember to leave tracks of your thinking as you read each text. What stands out? What questions are raised? What does this text seem to be about? What big ideas are you thinking about as you read? After you've read, what are you left wondering about? Evidence of your thinking should be displayed on each of these texts."

Give students time to read independently and actively engage with each text. The time frame will vary based on the number of texts in the set, the experience of the readers, and the amount of time you can allocate for this exercise. Reading can be done in school or assigned for homework. Sonja set aside classroom time for students to read texts independently. She wanted to monitor her students' progress and encourage students to show evidence of their close reading by marking the texts with their initial ideas and reactions.

When her students had finished reading each of the texts, Sonja asked them to use a graphic organizer to organize their ideas about each text, capture their "tracks," and mull over their thinking. Once these graphic organizers were completed, her students returned to their small groups to discuss their ideas. These discussions centered on general questions such as, *What did you notice? What did you feel? What issues were raised?* Alyssa gathered all of her annotations for each text into one location (see Figure 5.6).

Text	Annotations
On Turning Ten by Billy Collins	In the poem "On Turning Ten" by Billy Collins, the author describes having more responsibility and letting go of childhood comes with turning ten. The author uses very descriptive language to show readers that birthdays don't always meet expectations and that sometimes they can be upsetting. The character in the poem now realizes that his mistakes will have an impact on others
Edna Mae, First Lesson in Prejudice By Sandra Warren	In the poem "Edna Mae, First Lesson in Prejudice" by Sandra Warren, the author describes how life may not live up to our expectations. She describes how birthdays can teach people things about themselves and the world. The author also shows how birthdays can be disappointing sometimes.
Eleven By Sandra Cisneros	In the poem "Eleven" by Sandra Cisneros the author describes how birthdays don't take away from who you were, but they add on to who you are. The author of "Eleven" describes how as you get older, you still hang on to the part of you that's younger and that if sometimes you act on the part of you that's younger, that's ok. The character in the story has a really bad birthday, which is not what she thought it would be like.

Figure 5.6 Alyssa's Annotations

Listening to students' initial discussions, Sonja heard the following:

"These birthdays were depressing!"
"The authors make it seem like birthdays are bad."
"The characters are all disappointed on their birthdays."
"This is the opposite of what I feel about birthdays."

These initial thoughts served as a window into students' important first impressions and emerging ideas. This became a valuable resource for Sonja. She used it to inform and create instruction that helped her students analyze how these texts represent the authors'—and possibly the readers'—points of view and how the choices made by authors can help readers construct interpretations about theme.

Making Thesis Statements

Sonja took a few minutes to address the entire class.

"After spending time with each group, I noticed that you've generated several ideas about these texts. The ideas I heard included reactions about the tone of the texts and the author's point of view, the mood and how these texts made you feel, and general ideas about the topic of birthdays. I'd like you to analyze these texts by closely examining them—and your thinking about each of these texts—on your graphic organizer. Interpret these texts by writing down one or two big ideas in your reader's notebook that seem to represent all of these texts."

For students who seem stuck and are having difficulty generating an idea, encourage them to revisit the texts and engage in further conversations with their group.

Birthdays can change you and open your eyes to thethe world.

Figure 5.7 Sample "Big Idea"

Once students have constructed an initial interpretation about theme, based on the text set, invite them to collect evidence that supports their ideas.

"Remember, you'll need evidence from each of the three texts, not just from one or two of them, in order to make the claim that this theme is represented in the entire text set. You'll need the strongest evidence, not simply any evidence, to support your interpretations."

Remind students to follow citation rules about using quotation marks and page numbers. Students may benefit from the use of a graphic organizer here to help them collect text evidence and then analyze the evidence to demonstrate how it supports their interpretations. The following graphic organizer shows Jacob's interpretation of a big idea in the text set, his selection of evidence, and his analysis (see Figure 5.8 and the blank template toward the end of this chapter, Figure 5.20).

Big Idea: Birthdays and getting older can be something other than what you expect it to be.

Text	Evidence **Which** details best support your interpretation?	Analysis **How** does this evidence support your interpretation?
On Turning Ten by Billy Collins	"It is time to say goodbye to imaginary friends, time to turn the first big number."	Birthdays can be about leaving behind childish things. This means you can't dress up and have fun with make-belive friends.
Edna Mae, First Lesson in Prejudice By Sandra Warren	"We sat down on the steps and waited and waited. Edna Mae began to cry." (pg. 47)	Birthdays aren't always how we imagine them to be. They can be sad and disapointing.
Eleven By Sandra Cisneros	"You open your eyes and everything is just like yesterday, only it's today. And you don't feel eleven at all. You feel like you're still ten."	Birthdays can be dissapointing and you don't nesessarily feel like your new age.

Figure 5.8 Jacob's Interpretation

Earlier in this chapter, we used the example of *Star Wars* and an eight-year-old's birthday party as a way of understanding and identifying theme. We shared that themes emerge when we pay careful attention to details, such as people/characters, objects, setting, etc., and when we note patterns, such as repeated images, phrases, and emotions. With students' completed graphic organizers in hand, invite them to examine the evidence for their work. "Look at the evidence you've collected. Do you notice any patterns? Which ideas repeat? What does this evidence seem to be about? Name the thread(s) that seem to tie these texts together. Jot down the ideas that are beginning to emerge for you." Encourage students to share their ideas in their small groups. The goal is to generate new ideas and to receive feedback about ideas that are not substantiated by the texts. Repeated ideas students noticed in the text set include:

sadness	life lessons	disappointment	change
realization	responsibility	maturity	growing up

Revising Thesis Statements

Students have been provided with a great deal of scaffolds throughout this lesson that will support their work in identifying and interpreting a theme across text sets. Ask students to return to their reader's notebooks and work independently to respond to the following prompt:

> "What theme about birthdays have you identified in the text set? Remember that a theme is a thread that runs throughout a text that evokes an emotional response within the reader. You should feel strongly about your ideas. If you don't, you probably have not identified a theme. Use the evidence you've collected and the patterns you've noticed to strengthen your interpretation."

Students may return to the process of generating more ideas, rethinking, or experimenting using the Interpretation Framework. The following are examples of theme statements written by students who revised their claims:

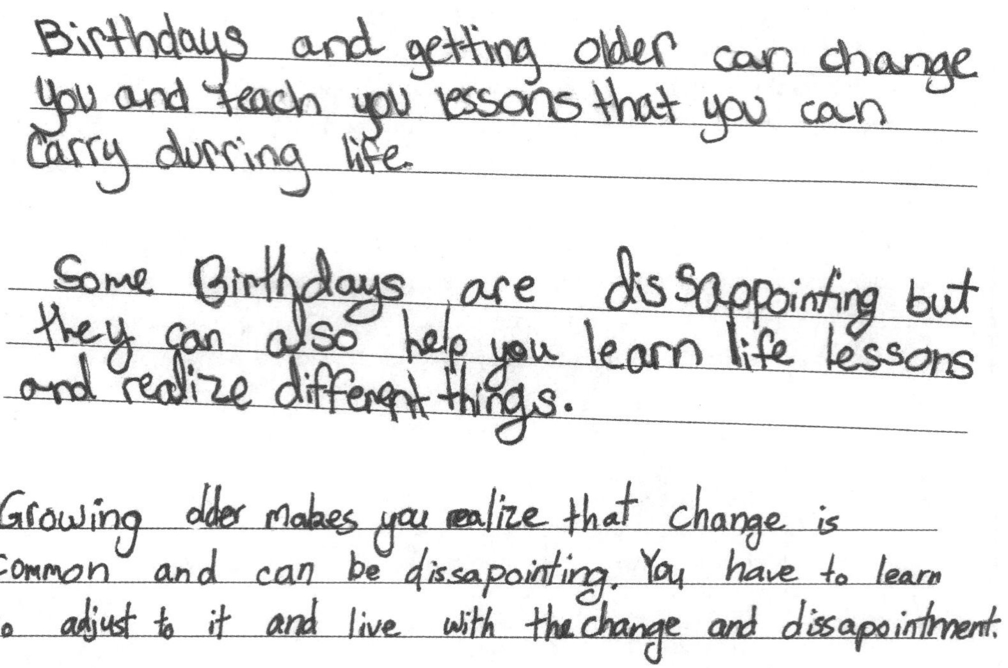

Birthdays and getting older can change you and teach you lessons that you can carry durring life.

Some Birthdays are dissapointing but they can also help you learn life lessons and realize different things.

Growing older makes you realize that change is common and can be dissapointing. You have to learn to adjust to it and live with the change and dissapointment.

Figure 5.9 Students' Thesis Statements

Constructing Written Responses to a Text Set

The work students have done in the previous section has prepared them to construct extended responses that support their interpretation of a theme from a text set. To construct their responses, students will need to attend to details of the text in ways that demonstrate their understanding of literary elements such as those discussed in this book (figurative language; mood, atmosphere, and tone; multiple perspectives; symbolism, etc.). As students attend to these elements and bring them together, they ground their ideas in the texts, reveal the authors' deeper messages, and respond based on their own life experiences. It is this connection between themes in a text and students' own experiences that make their interpretations powerful.

You might begin by encouraging students to note the mood of these texts and to consider how the authors created that mood and why. A close examination of the texts and the details within them helps readers unearth answers to this question. For example, ask students to consider the authors' use of physical reactions to birthdays in each text and how this helps to create mood. Model this process using one of the texts.

"I notice that in the poem 'On Turning Ten,' right away, the author compares a tenth birthday to an illness. Billy Collins turns my attention to this idea of sickness associated with this birthday with the phrase 'it makes me feel like I'm coming down with something, something worse than any stomach ache.' Comparing this birthday with a kind of sickness evokes a powerful feeling of dread. This is a very different perspective on birthdays. It sharply contrasts with what many people may typically associate with birthdays. I'm wondering, why is this a sad birthday? And have I ever felt similarly on my birthday? If so, why? Both Sandra Cisneros and Sandra Warren include physical reactions by the characters—specifically, crying—in their writing. As you examine the details of each of the texts further, think about the physical reactions the authors draw upon over others and why. How do these authors use physical reactions to create mood in these texts, and how does this support your ideas about theme?"

Sixth graders responded by writing about theme using a text set on birthdays (see Figures 5.10 and 5.11).

In the texts, the authors all talk about how birthdays are about realizing that when you get older, your perspective of the world can change. The three birthday related texts are the opposite of a sterio type birthday which is thought to have things like party hats and balloons. The texts talk about the reality of growing up.

In the text, On Turning Ten, by Billy Collins, Billy Collins writes about how when you're ten, you need to become more mature. He writes that when you grow up, you need to let go of your past. Finally, his writing is about how when you grow up, you look at the world differently.

(continues)

Figure 5.10 Doug's Interpretation of Theme Across Texts

In *Edna Mae: First Lesson in Prejudice*, by Sandra Warren, Edna Mae and her friend realize the reality of life. The author's writing shows how it was to have a birthday when African-Americans weren't being treated the same as white people. Edna Mae realizes that her view of the world would have to change.

Finally, in *Eleven* by Sandra Cisneros, the character in the writing, Rachel realizes that when she gets older, she doesn't lose part of herself, but she adds onto who she is. She thinks that when she is eleven, she is also all of the years before it. Her attitude can be negative because she realizes that she also can act like she did when she was in her younger ages like 3, 2, and 1.

All of the texts are different from the "typical birthday." *On Turning Ten*, *Edna Mae: First Lesson in Prejudice*, and *Eleven* all show how birthdays can be about your perspective changes when you get older. This is different from the "typical birthday" because with all of the laughter, cake, party hats, and fun, people don't really think about how they change as a person. Maybe, people should try to change what they think a "typical birthday" is.

Figure 5.10 Doug's Interpretation of Theme Across Texts *(continued)*

In the three texts Eleven, On Turning Ten, and Edna Mae: First Lesson in Prejudice the authors write about how birthdays can be a disappointment. Sandra Cisneros, (Eleven) Billy Collins, (On Turning Ten) and Sandra Warren (Edna Mae) describe how birthdays don't always live up to our expectations. However, they can be a time to open our eyes to the world, and learn to accept change and difference in it.

In the poem On Turning Ten Billy Collins describes what turning ten is like from the perspective of a soon-to-be ten-year old. The author describes feeling upset and depressed about turning ten. He feels that turning ten is the age where you have to learn to grow up and be mature. He has also realized that ten is when you are forced into the real world, and things will no longer be sugar-coated. Billy Collins also brings up that part of being ten is letting go of childhood and hanging onto responsibilities.

In the second text, Eleven by Sandra Cisneros the character Rachel learns that people will sometimes rain on your parade, and ruin a perfectly good day. The author describes Rachel's birthday as a ordinary day at school. Maybe even worse than an ordinary day. Rachel is so upset she begins to cry, in front of everyone. However, unlike the boy in On Turning Ten she realizes that birthdays do not take away, but add on to who you were, when you were younger. She believes that if you must act on the part of you that's younger, that's okay, because underneath the year that makes you older, you are younger.

In the third text, Edna Mae: First Lesson in Prejudice Sandra Warren describes a disappointing

(continues)

Figure 5.11 Alyssa's Interpretation of Theme Across Texts

birthday party from the perspective of Edna Mae's best friend. Edna Mae builds up her excitement when she talks to all of her friends about her birthday party. Unfortunately, the day of the party, the only one at Edna Mae's party is her best friend. Later, when her Mom picked the character up, she learned that nobody attended the party because of Edna Mae's race. At that moment, the girl fills with anger at the girls because they made Edna Mae cry at her birthday party. The girl later realizes that in reality people and the world can be cruel and unfair even to people who deserve better treatment.

Across these three texts, all of the authors show that life often will not live up to our hopes and dreams. Unlike how birthdays are usually characterized; all three characters had birthdays were not magical or special in any sort of way. In all of these texts the characters learn about the real world, and how to accept it the way it is.

Figure 5.11 Alyssa's Interpretation of Theme Across Texts *(continued)*

The Interpretation Framework Process

GENERATING IDEAS: Ask students to review their thinking about the texts to generate ideas about theme: "Some of you have identified change, realization, or disappointment as a theme. Now I'd like you to find some text evidence to support your answer and develop your ideas about theme." When generating ideas, remind students to look across *all* of the texts in a text set. Summarize for students that theme is "a thread that runs throughout a text that evokes an emotional response within the reader. A theme is comprised of abstract nouns and phrases and expresses universal ideas." Students may move directly from generating ideas to either rethinking or experimenting in the Interpretation Framework.

RETHINKING: When students look across multiple texts, they may discover that their initial ideas might work well for one text but not for all. Remind students that there can be more than one theme in a text and that it is important to explore multiple possibilities rather than settling in on a flawed or weak idea.

EXPERIMENTING: Encourage students to find the strongest text evidence to support their claims about a theme. Remind them to consider texts in their entirety, rather than just focusing on one paragraph or chapter. To strengthen claims about themes, students will need to select text evidence from the beginning, middle, and end of a text.

Strategies for Novice Readers

You may find that young readers have a difficult time determining theme in a text. At first, they may give summaries instead of finding a big idea. The following shows the work of a third grader who wrote about a theme in the book *Wilma Unlimited* by Kathleen Krull (see Figure 5.12).

We helped this writer through the process by guiding her to think about the powerful emotions that are woven throughout the text. Her second attempt moves her closer to writing about theme (see Figure 5.13).

Finally, we encouraged the student to think about the author's main point along with the powerful emotions she experienced as a reader of this text in order to construct an interpretation of theme (see Figure 5.14).

Wilma Rudolph was
born on June 23, 1940
in st. bethlehem   tennessee.
When she was littel,
she got polio which twisted her
left her left leg
paralyzed. She needed
a brace on her leg.
Her and her mom
would get on the
bus and go to a
hospital 50 miles
away in Nashville.
A medical student
would push her
leg in slow sercoms. circle
It hurt but she
was determined to
walk even though the
Doctors said she

Figure 5.12 Olivia's First Attempt When Writing About Theme

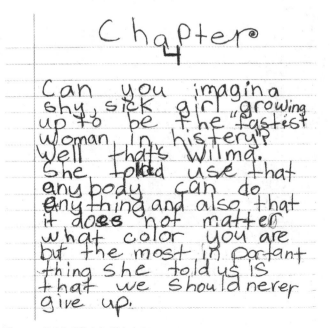

Chapter 2

Im

Wilma was so determendtoa that she did her exsersizeis to make her leg stronger alot more. One day at church even though she wasn't sopos to wilma stayed outside till everybody got in. Then she took of her brace and started to walk in. At first she was a little wabily but then she got used to it. After that day She still didhade to use the brace but not so much she was allowed to take the brace off. It was a mericol. miracle

Then 2 years later

Figure 5.13 Olivia's Second Attempt

Chapter 4

Can you imagina shy, sick girl growing up to be the "fastest woman in histery"? Well thats wilma. She tolked use that anybody can do anything and also that it does not matter what color you are but the most important thing she told us is that we should nerer give up.

Figure 5.14 Olivia's Third Attempt

Using the concept of birthdays or graduations is also an effective way to help novice students begin to think about theme. You may begin by asking students to brainstorm what comes to mind when you think about the word *graduation*. After giving students time to generate a few ideas, sum up some of the conversations you've overheard. Say to students:

"Each of you has likely experienced a graduation in your life. The idea of an important ceremony with caps and gowns, music and marching, certificates and diplomas may come to mind. You may think about leaving one school and going to the next, beginning the next grade, saying good-bye to old friends and making new ones. While a variety of different thoughts and images may come to mind, we can also think about a thread that runs through the idea of graduation. This thread, or theme, can tie up some of the emotions you may have felt and explain why you felt that way."

Ask students to discuss some of the feelings they've experienced around the idea of graduation and to organize their thinking by creating a chart with the class (see Figure 5.15).

This teaching strategy breaks down the process of identifying themes by inviting students to name their feelings around a topic, explain why they have those feelings, and ultimately describe a theme that corresponds to their ideas (see Figure 5.21 for a blank template of this chart).

Next, discuss the idea of universal themes with your students. You might say to your students, "Look at the themes we have generated on our chart. We call these *universal themes* because we may see them over and over in the texts we read and also in the world. While a particular universal theme will not be in *every* text, you will see it more than once. I've read that, 'A theme is an idea that is true in many places, in the stories we read and the lives we live.' (Calkins

Feelings/Emotions	Why?	Theme
Example • Sad	• Leaving friends • Leaving teachers • Leaving familiar place • New responsibilities	• Loneliness • Friendship • Saying good-bye
• Exciting	• New school • New grade • New friends	• Starting over • Moving forward
• Fear	• New teachers • New school • Different/harder work	• Facing the unknown • Accepting change

Figure 5.15 Theme Chart: Graduations

2010, p. 165). Can anyone name a theme from our chart that they've seen somewhere else?" Conversations like this can help teachers front-load students with universal themes. That way, as students read, they will have a frame of reference and a list of themes to refer to. Three lists of themes are located at the end of this chapter (see Figures 5.22–5.24). Choose the one that feels appropriate for your class and share it with your students.

If . . . Try . . .

HELPING NOVICE READERS CREATE INTERPRETATIONS ABOUT THEME

If . . .	Try . . .
Students cannot identify a theme in the text . . .	First, model for your students how to identify a theme. Use a text that they are familiar with and think aloud with questions such as: "What issues are raised? What does this text seem to be about? What are the big ideas? What am I left wondering or feeling after I read this text?" Give your students a copy of a theme list. Encourage them to try different themes and see which ones fit the best.
Students cannot identify text evidence to support their claim about theme . . .	Brainstorm the types of evidence students should be looking for in order to support their claim about theme. They are looking for multiple pieces of evidence *across a text* that shows the theme. Therefore, they should be looking for examples in the beginning, middle, and end of the text. In addition, model how to find characters' actions or reactions that *show* the theme. You may want to make a chart that has different examples of evidence related to characters that show theme (characters' actions, responses, reflections, realizations, initial feelings, turning points, etc.). Types of evidence include direct quotations, paraphrasing scenes or paragraphs, and a summary of chapters and even the entire text.
Students are having difficulty honing their interpretations about theme . . .	First, have your students write down (perhaps on a sticky note) their claim. Next, ask your students to think about the author's purpose. For example, a student's claim might be "a theme in this text is growing up." As you guide your student to think about the author's purpose and reasons for writing about this theme, your student might write: "The author writes about people not wanting to grow up because things change." This can lead your student to hone their initial claim and create a thesis statement such as, "Growing up can be difficult because things change and are unpredictable."

Figure 5.16 If . . . Try . . .

Strategies for Advanced Readers

Encourage students to examine figurative language and symbolism used in these texts in order to develop their ideas about theme. For example, you might model the following for students:

> "In the poem 'On Turning Ten,' Billy Collins writes 'It seems only yesterday I used to believe there was nothing under my skin but light. If you cut me I could shine. But now when I fall upon the sidewalks of life, I skin my knees. I bleed.' How does figurative language used in this text support your ideas about theme? In 'Eleven' by Sandra Cisneros, the red sweater is prominent throughout the text. As a result of reading closely, we can see that this isn't simply a sweater. How does Cisneros use symbolism in ways that connect to theme?"

Noticing and noting the authors' use of mood, figurative language, and symbolism in each of these texts and how this connects to theme will help students construct powerful extended responses. Challenge students to apply these skills with longer texts, such as the ones they read in their book club or independent reading novels.

If . . . Try . . .

HELPING ADVANCED READERS CREATE INTERPRETATIONS ABOUT THEME

If . . .	Try . . .
Students cannot locate multiple pieces of text evidence . . .	Brainstorm and list the different types of evidence students might look for when searching for evidence of theme. This list might include: characters' action and reactions, turning points in the plot, big and small realizations, evidence of character, or conflict development (beginning, middle, and end).
Students are making claims that are strong but could be even stronger . . .	Encourage students to make connections between themes in the text and themes in the world today. What does the author want the reader to think about and consider?
Students are forming a strong claim and finding strong evidence but not rethinking . . .	Have your students consider alternate themes by referring to the themes list. Then have your students rule out alternate themes. It is equally important for students to recognize themes that do not work and aren't as strong as their claim in order to make their work even stronger.

Figure 5.17 If . . . Try . . .

Planning a Year of Teaching Theme

You can begin teaching theme the first week of school through picture books, poetry, etc., or you can begin teaching theme later in the school year; we have done it both ways. Teaching theme begins with a discussion of what *theme* means and why authors create it. Once you have launched your theme study, you can return to it over and over in your reading curriculum. The more practice students have identifying themes and creating interpretations, the better. If you choose to teach theme across the school year, your lessons might look like the following:

Theme Lessons Across the School Year

September: Assess your students' understanding of theme. Introduce what theme means and why good readers think about themes in the texts they read. Provide students with a list of themes so they have examples. Create a chart with "plot" and "theme."

October: Model for your students how they can generate initial claims about themes in the books they are reading. Help students locate text evidence for their claims by making a chart about the kinds of evidence they might look for.

November: Help students find the best text evidence that supports their claims about theme, and have students rank order their evidence from weakest to strongest.

December: In small groups or book clubs, remind students to rethink their claims. This may look like students finding alternate claims and weighing which claim is the strongest, based on the evidence they have found. Continue having students look for themes in each text they read.

January: Challenge students to look for themes across texts. What themes do they see reoccurring? Why do authors choose these themes? How do the authors present them differently?

February: Connect theme to other literary elements such as symbolism, multiple perspectives, and tone. How do these pieces connect and work together to relay the author's big ideas?

March: Students should be able to identify themes in texts and make initial claims. Focus on students' ability to journey through the Interpretation Framework on their own. Can they generate ideas about theme, experiment with evidence, and rethink their claims?

April: This month, focus on students' ability to craft and hone thesis statements about theme. Are they specific? Do they have strong text evidence to support their thesis statement?

May: As your students locate themes in their texts, differentiate your instruction to deepen both your novice and advanced readers' thinking by using the suggestions in the If . . . Try . . . boxes.

June: End your year of teaching theme by reviewing the Interpretation Framework process.

Text/Movie	Plot	Theme

Figure 5.18

TEXT: _____

Events/Plot	Themes

Figure 5.19

TEXT: _____

Text	Evidence Which details best support your interpretation?	Analysis How does this evidence support your interpretation?

Figure 5.20

TEXT: _____

Feelings/Emotions You Feel When Reading the Text	Why?/Text Evidence	Theme

Figure 5.21

Themes List
friendship
freedom
fairness
love
kindness
cooperation
family
bravery
sadness
loneliness
determination
loyalty

Figure 5.22

Themes List	
friendship	inequality
freedom	injustice
fairness	growing up
love	independence
kindness	self-respect
cooperation	working together
family	segregation
bravery	discrimination
sadness	good versus evil
loneliness	perseverance
determination	responsibility
loyalty	maturity
	greed

Figure 5.23

Themes List		
friendship	inequality	racial inequality
freedom	injustice	transitions
fairness	growing up	fighting for what's right
love	independence	overcoming obstacles
kindness	self-respect	oppression
cooperation	working together	repression
family	segregation	gender bias
bravery	discrimination	power
sadness	good versus evil	privilege
loneliness	perseverance	morality
determination	responsibility	breaking/repeating cycles
loyalty	maturity	diversity
	greed	

Figure 5.24

Concluding Thoughts

As both teachers and learners, we understand the relentless pursuit of educators to design and deliver instruction that extends students' learning to new and higher levels. Throughout this book, we have shared some of our real-life experiences as teachers and the ways in which we've collaborated to extend our own learning. We think of this book as both a mirror and a window. It represents our ongoing reflections on the process of helping students to construct interpretations about texts, and, we hope, provides a view of ways in which to make this work more concrete and accessible to all students.

At a time when the Common Core State Standards encourages teachers to focus their reading instruction on ways that may confine students to the "four corners" of the text, we need to be mindful of the importance of bringing our readers' lived experiences, feelings, and their knowledge as readers to our teaching of reading. It is important to balance providing analytical tools and strategies students need in order to read texts closely and make meaning from them, while understanding that *no one* can analyze or interpret texts without bringing themselves to the text.

We certainly realize that the process of reading involves the culmination of many skills that are enacted simultaneously, rather than in isolation. However, in order to help students strengthen their interpretations of texts, they'll need a solid understanding of concepts and literary elements that can help them generate, experiment, and revise their ideas. Focused attention around these elements can provide instructional supports for students as they navigate challenging texts and make meaning of them. Such support can help readers construct powerful interpretations each time they journey through and across texts.

References

Adler, David. 2000. *America's Champion Swimmer: Gertrude Ederle*. Orlando, FL: Harcourt.

Ada, Alma F. 1998. "The Bats." *Under the Royal Palms: A Childhood in Cuba*. New York: Simon and Schuster.

Ahlberg, Allan, and Jane Ahlberg. 2001. *The Jolly Postman*. New York: Little Brown Books.

Allington, Richard L. 2012. *What Really Matters for Struggling Readers: Designing Research-Based Programs*. 3rd ed. Boston, MA: Pearson.

Alvarez, Julia. 2002. *How Tia Lola Came To (Visit) Stay*. New York: Yearling.

Angelou, Maya. 1993. *Life Doesn't Frighten Me*. New York: Stewart, Tobori, and Chang.

Applegate, Katherine. 2012. *The One and Only Ivan*. New York: HarperCollins.

Babbitt, Natalie. 1974. *Tuck Everlasting*. New York: Ferrar, Straus, and Giroux.

Beers, Kylene, and Robert E. Probst. 2012. *Notice and Note: Strategies for Close Reading*. Portsmouth, NH: Heinemann.

Bomer, Randy, and Katherine Bomer. 2001. *For a Better World: Reading and Writing for Social Action*. Portsmouth, NH: Heinemann.

Bradby, Marie. 1995. *More Than Anything Else*. New York: Orchard Books.

Browne, Anthony. 1992. *Zoo*. New York: Alfred A. Knopf.

Bunting, Eve. 1991. *Fly Away Home*. New York: Houghton Mifflin Company.

———. 1994. *Smoky Night*. Orlando, FL: Harcourt.

Buyea, Rob. 2010. *Because of Mr. Terupt*. New York: Random House.

Calkins, Lucy. 2000. *The Art of Teaching Reading*. Boston, MA: Pearson.

Calkins, Lucy, and Mary Ehrenworth. 2010. *Tackling Complex Texts: Historical Fiction in Book Clubs, Volume One: Synthesizing Perspectives*. Portsmouth, NH: Heinemann.

———. 2010. *Tackling Complex Texts: Historical Fiction in Book Clubs, Volume Two: Interpretation and Critical Reading*. Portsmouth, NH: Heinemann.

Calkins, Lucy, Mary Ehrenworth, and Christopher Lehman. 2012. *Pathways to the Common Core: Accelerating Achievement*. Portsmouth, NH: Heinemann.

Cannon, Janell. 1993. *Stellaluna*. Boston, MA: Houghton Mifflin.

Chall, Marsha Wilson. 1992. *Up North at the Cabin*. New York: HarperCollins.

Chavez, Cesar. 2002. *Harvesting Hope: The Story of Cesar Chavez*. San Diego, CA: Harcourt.

Cisneros, Sandra. 1997. *Los Pelitos*. New York: Dragonfly Books.

———. 1991. "Eleven." *Woman Hollering Creek and Other Stories*. New York: Vintage.

Clements, Andrew. 1996. *Frindle*. New York: Simon and Schuster.

Collins, Billy. 2002. "On Turning Ten." *Sailing Alone Around the Room: New and Selected Poems*. New York: Random House.

Conkling, Winifred. 2011. *Sylvia & Aki*. New York: Random House.

Cox, Lynne. 2008. *Grayson*. Boston, MA: Mariner Books.

Crandell, Rachel. 2002. *Hands of the Maya: Villagers at Work and Play*. New York: Henry Holt and Company.

Creech, Sharon. 1994. *Walk Two Moons*. New York: HarperCollins.

———. 1998. *Bloomability*. New York: HarperCollins.

———. 2005. *Granny Torrelli Makes Soup*. New York: HarperCollins.

Curtis, Christopher P. 1999. *Bud Not Buddy*. New York: Random House.

Daniels, Harvey "Smokey," and Nancy Steineke. 2011. *Texts and Lessons for Content-Area Reading*. Portsmouth, NH: Heinemann.

———. 2013. *Texts and Lessons for Teaching Literature*. Portsmouth, NH: Heinemann.

Davis, Judy, and Sharon Hill. 2003. "My Grandmother's Hair," by Cynthia Rylant, in *The No-Nonsense Guide to Teaching Writing*. Portsmouth, NH: Heinemann.

de la Peña, Matt. 2011. *A Nation's Hope: The Story of Boxing Legend Joe Louis*. New York: Dial.

de Maupassant, Guy. 1997. "The Necklace." *The Best Short Stories: Guy de Maupassant*. London: Wordsworth Editions.

DiCamillo, Kate. 2001. *Because of Winn-Dixie*. Somerville, MA: Candlewick Press.

———. 2006. *Tiger Rising*. Somerville, MA: Candlewick Press.

Draper, Sharon M. 2012. *Out of My Mind*. New York: Atheneum Books for Young Readers.

Fleischman, Paul. 1988. *Joyful Noise: Poems for Two Voices*. New York: HarperCollins.

———. 1993. *Bull Run*. New York: HarperCollins.

———. 2002. *Weslandia*. Somerville, MA: Candlewick Press.

———. 2004. *Seedfolks*. New York: Harpercollins.

Flournoy, Valerie. *The Patchwork Quilt*. New York: Dial Books for Young Readers.

Fountas, Irene, and Gay Su Pinnell. 2006. *Teaching for Comprehending and Fluency: Thinking, Talking, and Writing About Reading K–8*. Portsmouth, NH: Heinemann.

Frost, Robert. 1995. "The Road Not Taken." *A Child's Anthology of Poetry*. Edited by Elizabeth Hauge Sword. New York: HarperCollins.

Garland, Sherry. 1997. *The Lotus Seed*. Orlando, FL: Voyager Books.

George, Jean Craighead. 1972. *Julie of the Wolves*. New York: HarperCollins.

———. *My Side of the Mountain*. New York: Puffin Books.

Harvey, Stephanie, and Anne Goudvis. 2000. *Strategies That Work: Teaching Comprehension to Enhance Understanding*. Portland, ME: Stenhouse Publishers.

Hazen, Barbara. 1979. *Tight Times*. New York: Penguin Books.

Hughes, Langston. 1994. "Harlem." *The Collected Poems of Langston Hughes*. New York: Vintage Books.

———. 1994. "Mother to Son." *The Dream Keeper and Other Poems*. New York: Random House.

———. 1996. "Early Autumn." *The Short Stories of Langston Hughes*. New York: Hill and Wang.

———. 1996. "Thank You, Ma'am." *The Short Stories of Langston Hughes*. Ramona Bass and Arnold Rampersad, eds. New York: Farrar, Straus, and Giroux.

If You Lived at the Time of . . . series. New York: Scholastic.

Hunter-Gault, Charlayne. 2012. *To the Mountaintop: My Journey Through the Civil Rights Movement*. New York: Flash Point Publishers.

Jacobs, William W. 2003. "The Monkey's Paw." *Great Stories of Suspense and Adventure*. Berlin, NJ: Townsend Press.

Jones, Stephanie. 2006. *Girls, Social Class, and Literacy: What Teachers Can Do to Make a Difference*. Portsmouth, NH: Heinemann.

Judge, Lita. 2007. *One Thousand Tracings: Healing the Wounds of World War II*. New York: Hyperion Books.

Keene, Ellin Oliver, and Susan Zimmermann. 1997. *Mosaic of Thought: Teaching Comprehension in a Reader's Workshop*. Portsmouth, NH: Heinemann.

King, Martin L. Jr. 1963. "I Have a Dream" speech, given at the March on Washington for Jobs and Freedom, Washington, DC, August 28. Available at http://www.nobelprize.org/nobel_prizes/peace/laureates/1964/king-wall.html. Accessed 12/9/2013.

Krull, Kathleen. 1996. *Wilma Unlimited*. Orlando, FL: Harcourt.

Lasseter, John et al. 1995. *Toy Story*. Burbank, CA: Buena Vista Pictures.

Lazarus, Emma. 2005. "The Great Colossus." *Emma Lazarus: Selected Poems*. Edited by John Hollander. New York: Literary Classics.

Lee-Tai, Amy. 2006. *A Place Where Sunflowers Grow*. San Francisco, CA: Children's Book Press.

Lehman, Christopher, and Kate Roberts. 2014. *Falling in Love with Close Reading*. Portsmouth, NH: Heinemann.

Levine, Ellen. 2007. *Henry's Freedom Box*. New York: Scholastic Press.

Lewison, Mitzi, Amy Seely Flint, and Katie Van Sluys. 2002. "Taking on critical literacy: The journey of newcomers and novices." *Language Arts* 79 (5): 382–393.

Lin, Grace. 2009. *Where the Mountain Meets the Moon*. New York: Little Brown Books.

Lincoln, Abraham. "The Gettysburg Address" speech, given at the dedication of the Soldiers' National Cemetery in Gettysburg, Pennsylvania, November 19. Available at http://abrahamlincolnonline.org/lincoln/speeches/gettysburg.htm. Accessed 10/10/2013.

Lord, Bette Bao. 2003. *In the Year of the Boar and Jackie Robinson*. New York: HarperCollins.

Lord, Cynthia. 2006. *Rules*. New York: Scholastic Press.

Lowry, Lois. 1989. *Number the Stars*. New York: Houghton Mifflin.

———. 1993. *The Giver*. New York: Random House.

Lyon, George E. 1999. "Where I'm From." *Where I'm From, Where Poems Come From*. Spring, TX: Absey and Co.

McDonald, Megan. 2000. *Judy Moody: Was in a Mood*. Somerville, MA: Candlewick Press.

Minkoff, Rob and Roger Allers et al. 1994. *The Lion King*. Burbank, CA: Buena Vista Pictures.

Mochizuki, Ken. 1997. *Passage to Freedom: The Sugihara Story*. New York: Lee and Low Books.

Mohr, Nicholassa. 1975. "The Wrong Lunch Line." *El Bronx Remembered: A Novella and Stories*. New York: HarperCollins.

Naylor, Phyllis R. 2000. *Shiloh*. New York: Aladdin Paperbacks.

Obama, Barack. 2009. "Inaugural Address" speech, given at the 2009 Presidential Inauguration at the Capitol Building, Washington, DC, January 20. Available at http://www.nytimes.com/2009/01/20/us/politics/20text-obama.html?pagewanted=all&_r=0. Accessed 1/6/2014.

O'Flaherty, Liam. 1937. "His First Flight." *The Short Stories of Liam O'Flaherty*. London: J. Cape.

Palacio, R. J. 2012. *Wonder*. New York: Random House.

Parish, Peggy. 2012. *Amelia Bedelia*. *I Can Read* Series Book Level 2. New York: Greenwillow Books.

Paulsen, Gary. 1987. *Hatchet*. New York: Aladdin Paperbacks.

Perkins, Mitali. 2008. *Rickshaw Girl*. Watertown, MA: Charlesbridge.

Perry, Katy. 2012. "Firework." *Teenage Dream*. Los Angeles, CA: Capitol Records.

Poe, Edgar A. (1843) 1983. "The Tell-Tale Heart." *The Tell-Tale Heart*. New York: Random House.

Polacco, Patricia. 1998. *Thank You Mr. Falkner*. New York: Penguin Putnam Books.

———. 2001. *The Keeping Quilt*. New York: Aladdin Paperbacks.

Porter, Pamela. 2005. *The Crazy Man*. Toronto, ON: Groundwood Books.

Rappaport, Doreen, and Bryan Collier. 2012. *Martin's Big Words*. New York: Hyperion Books.

Ringgold, Faith. 1998. *My Dream of Martin Luther King*. New York: Dragonfly Books.

Raven, Margot. 2008. *Night Boat to Freedom*. New York: Square Fish.

Rumford, James. 2008. *Silent Music: A Story of Baghdad*. New York: Running Brook Press.

Ryan, Pam M. 2002. *When Marian Sang: The True Recital of Marian Anderson*. New York: Scholastic Press.

————. 2002. *Esperanza Rising*. New York: Scholastic.

Rylant, Cynthia. 1985. *Every Living Thing*. New York: Simon and Schuster.

Santiago, Esmeralda. "How to Eat a Guava." *When I Was Puerto Rican*. Cambridge, MA: Da Capo Press.

Santman, Donna. 2005. *Shades of Meaning: Comprehension and Interpretation in Middle School*. Portsmouth, NH: Heinemann.

Schotter, Roni. 2000. *F is for Freedom*. CreateSpace Independent Publishing Platform.

Scieszka, Jon. 1989. *The True Story of the Three Little Pigs*. New York: Puffin Books.

————. 1993. *The Stinky Cheese Man and Other Fairly Stupid Tales*. New York: Viking Juvenile.

Seuss, Dr. 1969. *Horton Hatches the Egg*. New York: Random House.

————. 1971. *The Lorax*. New York: Random House.

Smith, Samuel F. 1831. "My Country, 'Tis of Thee." *Wikipedia*, last modified December 26, 2013, http://en.wikipedia.org/wiki/My_Country,_'Tis_of_Thee.

Spinelli, Jerry. 1990. *Maniac Magee*. New York: Little Brown Books for Young Readers.

Stanton, Andrew et al. 2003. *Finding Nemo*. Burbank, CA: Buena Vista Pictures.

Steele, Phillip. 2009. *The Aztec News*. Somerville, MA: Candlewick Press.

————. 2009. *The Egyptian News*. Somerville, MA: Candlewick Press.

Stone, Tanya L. 2009. *Almost Astronauts: Thirteen Women Who Dared to Dream*. Somerville, MA: Candlewick Press.

Taylor, Theodore. 1968. *The Cay*. New York: Random House.

Taylor, Mildred. 1976. *Roll of Thunder, Hear My Cry*. New York: Puffin Books.

Teague, Mark. 2003. *Dear Mrs. LaRue*. New York: Scholastic.

The Beatles. 1969. "Here Comes the Sun." *Abbey Road*. London: EMI.

Time for Kids. 1995. New York: Time Brand.

Trousdale, Gary, and Kirk Wise et al. 1991. *Beauty and the Beast*. Burbank, CA: Buena Vista Pictures.

Tsuchiya, Yukio. 1988. *Faithful Elephants*. New York: Houghton Mifflin Company.

Uchida, Yoshiko. 1993. *The Bracelet*. London: Philomel.

Warren, Sandra. 1999. "Edna Mae: First Lesson in Prejudice," from *Chicken Soup for the Kid's Soul: 101 Stories of Courage, Hope, and Laughter for Kids Ages 8–12*. New York: Scholastic.

Wiles, Deborah. 2001. *Freedom Summer*. New York: Atheneum Books for Young Readers.

Winter, Jeanette. 2008. *Wangari's Trees of Peace: A True Story from Africa*. Orlando, FL: Harcourt Publications.

Van Allsburg, Chris. 1991. *The Wretched Stone*. New York: Houghton Mifflin Company.

————. 1992. *The Widow's Broom*. New York: Houghton Mifflin Company.

White, E. B. 1970. *Trumpet of the Swan*. New York: HarperCollins.

Woodson, Jacqueline. 2001. *The Other Side.* New York: Penguin Putnam Books for Young Readers.

———. 2012. *Each Kindness.* New York: Nancy Paulsen Books.

Wyeth, Sharon D. 2013. *The Granddaughter Necklace.* New York: Scholastic.

Yolen, Jane. 1987. *Owl Moon.* London: Philomel.

———. 1996. *Encounter.* Boston, MA: HMH Books.

You Wouldn't Want to Be series. New York: Scholastic.